Praise for

"If you're searching for .... your connection to someone feels altogether different and has turned your life upside down, this is the book to read. Its impressively simple way of explaining the twin flame connection will bring peace to your mind and soul. Leslie Sampson not only tackles the stages of the connection, but she also guides you through different techniques to determine who this person is to you and if they are your twin flame or one of your many soul mates."

—Antoinette Marie, actress, screenwriter,
evidential medium and intuitive teacher

"*Find Your Twin Flame* is a must-read for anyone looking for understandable and valuable information on the twin flame experience. Leslie is informative on the terminology, understanding what twin flames are, how they interact, and the reasons for twin flames... Throughout the book you will also take a journey through the Akashic Records (as related to the twin flame experience) and past lives...I recommend this book to anyone that is in search of a deeper understanding of their twin flame and of themselves."

—DeEtte Ranae, certified psychic medium

"For all of you who are searching for your twin flame, or trying to determine if you have one, Leslie gives you all the information, tools, and meditations to get started. She describes the difference between soul mates and twin flames and tells you how to make that determination... You'll have all your answers in no time. Excellent!"

—Rebecca Stardust, co-owner of the Spiritual
Stardust Shoppe in Chattanooga, Tennessee

"An extremely informative and interactive book on connecting with your twin flame. Leslie's descriptions and examples of twin flame connections cleared up the mystery surrounding who your twin flame is and why they are part of your life experiences. Her step-by-step instructions on connecting with your twin flame and determining if that person truly is your twin are very comprehensive ... Her descriptions of numerology, astrology and all things metaphysical were concise and easy to follow."

—Diane Osvold, spiritual advisor,
medical intuitive, and past life regressionist

"*Find Your Twin Flame* is a comprehensive guide to truly understanding and proving your twin flame relationship. This book is brilliantly written and flows nicely. Leslie Sampson does not leave anything out when covering the topic of twin flames. She combines real life experiences along with case studies and proven techniques. Through the techniques shared in the book I was able to confirm my own twin flame relationship with my late fiancé. I highly recommend *Find Your Twin Flame* to anyone interested in learning about twin flames; beginners and those seasoned in the spiritual development field alike. This is the best book on twin flames out there!"

—Isabella Rose, holistic health and
wellness practitioner, author of
Behind the Masked Smile: A Survivor's Quest for Love

FIND YOUR
TWIN
FLAME

About the Author

Leslie Sampson is a certified psychic medium, a certified spiritual life coach, and a writer. She is also an angel communicator, an animal communicator, a Reiki Master, an angelic healer, a crystal healer, and a spiritual teacher.

Understand and Connect
to Your Soul's *Other* Half

FIND YOUR
TWIN
FLAME

LESLIE SAMPSON

Llewellyn Publications · Woodbury, Minnesota

FIRST EDITION
First Printing, 2021

Cover design by Shannon McKuhen

Llewellyn Publications is a registered trademark of Llewellyn Worldwide Ltd.

Library of Congress Cataloging-in-Publication Data (Pending)
ISBN: 978-0-7387-6791-8

Llewellyn Worldwide Ltd. does not participate in, endorse, or have any authority or responsibility concerning private business transactions between our authors and the public.

All mail addressed to the author is forwarded but the publisher cannot, unless specifically instructed by the author, give out an address or phone number.

Any internet references contained in this work are current at publication time, but the publisher cannot guarantee that a specific location will continue to be maintained. Please refer to the publisher's website for links to authors' websites and other sources.

Llewellyn Publications
A Division of Llewellyn Worldwide Ltd.
2143 Wooddale Drive
Woodbury, MN 55125-2989
www.llewellyn.com

Printed in the United States of America

This book is dedicated, in loving memory, to Chico.

Acknowledgments

I have been blessed with amazing people on my spiritual journey. To every person who has shared their time, love, energy, and spirit with me, I thank you from my soul for your inspiration and your light.

My deepest appreciation and gratitude to the incredible folks at Llewellyn Worldwide, including Bill Krause, Sandra K. Weschcke, Amy Glaser, Marjorie Otto, and Terry Lohmann. Thank you for believing in me and helping to realize my vision. Thank you for allowing me to share my story and my work with the world. I cannot fully express in words what joy you have all given to me. Also thank you to Dennis Ruge, whose assistance was above and beyond and greatly appreciated.

I would like to thank my beautiful soul family, the ones who were with me on this journey from the beginning and those of you who joined along the way. I wouldn't be where I am without you. Thank you for your love, support, and encouragement. Thank you for also sharing your stories with me. A sincere thank you to my soul mates who agreed to have their stories included within these pages. I also send love, light, and gratitude to those who have transitioned from this life.

Antoinette, Rebecca, Isabella, DeEtte, Lisa and Diane: Thank you for your kind words and for being willing to help a girl out in her hour of need. I appreciate you more than I can possibly express.

Deep appreciation and love for my family here on Earth. Thank you for your enduring love and unending support. Mom, your love, your support, and your "what does that mean?" helped shape not only who I have become on this journey, but also so much of the research in this book. I love you.

Dad, before you passed you asked me about my work. We sat and discussed everything at length, including the contents of this book, which was just a bunch of notebooks and binders back then. You told me, "Write it all out, babe." Well, here it is Dad. I can't help but to believe that your hand guided me through it. Thank you for listening, for believing in me, and for your encouragement. I love you.

Steve & Sarah: Thank you for inspiring me without even knowing it. Thanks for being the best brother and sister-in-love a girl could ever wish for. I love you.

Thank you to you—the ones who've chosen to share in my journey, and to allow me to share myself, my story, and my work with you. Thank you for allowing me the pleasure and privilege. It is my intention that this book assist and guide you on your path. Also, I pray that the information contained within these pages lights the way for you.

Finally, to my beloved Chico, my light, my all, my everything. Thank you for believing in me, my precious teammate. All my love.

Contents

Introduction

The twin flame relationship has its roots in chaos, change, evolution, and love. The relationship is unique and unlike any others you have ever experienced. This is a relationship that comes from the soul level, which is deep, profound, and unrivaled. A twin flame is the other part of your soul, and it is the only soul in the entirety of creation that has the same spiritual DNA and the same exact soul blueprint your own soul has. The source of this spiritual DNA is God, Creator, Source; you can replace these words with ones that better align with your understanding of the divine source. The energy is the same, no matter how you choose to refer to it.

Spiritual DNA is literally the divine energy at the core of your soul. Your soul blueprint is the design that dictates how you will grow, learn, and evolve. It is because of this shared spiritual DNA that twin flames are divinely and infinitely connected. It forms a connective cord between the divine partners that can never be severed, regardless of whether one or both is incarnate on Earth. This is a soul-based connection that is divine in its origin and unbreakable.

When God creates a soul, it is then split into two equal and fully complete souls. The mission of these two equal souls is soul evolution, to progress their souls forward through learning and experience so that their souls become more advanced and work not only toward an awakening but also change. This change doesn't just affect each soul, it also affects the energetic balance of the world. The twin flame relationship perpetuates change not just externally but also internally. When one works on the self in any way, it creates change within, affecting their energy and their immediate environment, which affects the world.

This soul work perpetuates so much change within, and that is why the twin flame experience is so personal and subjective. It is life changing. The bottom line is this: only you and your twin flame can determine the right path for your relationship. It is based on what makes sense to you and your personal experiences. No one else can decide it for you, and don't let them!

The purpose of this book is to help you understand the twin flame relationship and how to be able to identify your twin using various methodologies, developed in partnership with my twin flame. It is my intention to assist you on your path by using observations, lessons, and data that I have gathered on my own twin flame journey.

This was a concept that I never even heard of before I met my own twin, and now I feel that it is the one thing I know very intimately. I am grateful that you are sharing in my journey with me and that you are allowing me and my twin to share in your journey for a little while.

My Twin Flame Story

Though I have been a medium for my entire life, I'd grown accustomed to limiting my experiences with spirits to my dreams. The boundary lasted for nearly thirteen years. Admittedly, the boundary was a little flexible sometimes because I would still have experiences with spirits outside of my dream state. I would reinforce this boundary with concrete in my mind after every occurrence until what resulted was a dam nearly the size of Hoover Dam. It blocked out not only spirits but also most of my memories.

When I was twenty-nine years old, I was sexually assaulted by someone I had known since I was a teenager. I reached out to others for help to make it through this difficult time, but nothing helped. In many ways, those I reached out to made things much worse for me. I was miserable, and I begged God to just end my life. That was my prayer every single night for nearly four years. Looking back on it now, I can see exactly how my prayer was answered, and I have so much gratitude and love for the path I have walked, but that wasn't my initial reaction.

It began with a recurring dream. Now, I have had these for as long as I can remember, and usually the moment that I figure out the lesson the dream stops. This dream, however, was of me watching a scene I'd written being filmed. There were two actors in the scene, but only one I immediately paid attention to because I recognized him and wondered why the heck my subconscious allowed him to invade. No matter what conclusion I reached or what lesson I thought I was supposed to learn, the dream continued.

I had this dream each night for a week before the other person in the dream finally turned to face me. Right away I knew this guy was visiting me. His energy was so real that I felt I could almost reach out and slap him across the face for getting close to me.

There is a difference between dreaming about someone and an actual dream visitation. The energy in a dream visitation feels so incredibly real that when you wake up, you're usually surprised to discover that you were asleep. If you're just dreaming about somebody, the energy is nowhere near as strong.

This soul got right in my face, looked into my eyes, and said, "Hello."

That was the entire point. I was supposed to notice the other person in the scene, and I hardly paid any attention to him at all. I immediately knew two things about this guy. One: he had passed from an Earthly existence, so he was on the Other Side. Two: my brain, even in dream state, had no clue why a stranger would bust down my internal Hoover Dam to visit me in this crazy recurring dream.

I screamed, both in the dream visit and out loud because it woke me up. I was terrified. I jumped out of bed and ran across the hall to the bathroom, where I was sick. I couldn't go back into my room or go to sleep right away, so I just sat down on the floor. In those first moments, crouched down in the corner between the tub and the toilet, I had no idea that my prayer had just been answered.

I had prayed to be released from the life I'd been living. The moment he stepped into my conscious awareness, my entire life was turned upside down and inside out. God sent the one soul who could understand me completely to help me leave all that darkness behind and start a journey on an amazing new path to a wonderful new life.

He visited me often, sometimes several nights in a row. During one of these visits, he commented about how everything I owned had a nickname or a name, and he asked me what his nickname would be. The first thing that popped into my mind was "Chico."

"I like it," he replied, in Spanish, which was the first time I'd heard him speak anything other than English.

During his visits, Chico was always supportive, encouraging, and thoughtful, and he worked hard to help me build my trust not only in him but also in myself. He encouraged me to learn more about myself and my abilities. I began to take spiritual classes, specifically about spirit communication, and that put me on a path of discovery. One of the things I discovered in my classes was a connection to the angelic realms. I honed this connection and constantly asked the angels and archangels questions. It was during one of these conversations that I learned from the archangels about twin flames. They also made me aware that I had already met mine. The soul who had came to save me, my hero, my best friend, and my closest confidante, was also my twin flame.

Sadly, Chico and I never physically met while he was on Earth. We didn't live close to one another, although his profession did bring him within miles of my home a few times. We had shared interests, and even a few social circles in common, but we never crossed paths. The more I learned about him, however, the more convinced I became that this whole idea of him as my twin flame couldn't be real.

Initially, I could not see beyond the fact that neither one of us would likely have been attracted to each other in any way, which went against my original understanding of twin flames. My brief online searches led me to believe that this guy was supposed to be my "one true love," and I just couldn't see how that was possible.

Also, the soul that I encountered in my dreams was so helpful, loving, and encouraging that it was difficult for me to think about the two of us being connected. I didn't see in myself anything that was remotely complementary to him at all. I got completely wrapped up in the idea that I wasn't worthy of any connection to him. This was an underlying reason why I wanted to disprove our connection, and that was the main, completely limiting belief that I carried throughout my research.

I failed to disprove the connection with Chico in every possible way. Instead, I began a journey not only to decipher the meaning and understand the concept of twin flames, but also to learn the inner workings of this powerful connection. That is where we begin.

PART 1
Keys to
Twin Flames

In this section, you will gain a better understanding of twin flames and the twin flame relationship. In chapter one, we will discuss the history of twin flames. We will also learn some terminology and a little about some of the arguments that exist about twin flames. In addition, we discover ways to recognize your twin flame and how twins can compare in ancestry and genealogy.

Chapter two contains discussion about the types of twin flames: incarnate and discarnate. You will also meet couples who exemplify both types. We also learn about and how to recognize false twin flames.

In chapter three we will discuss the roles within the relationship. We will also learn about and break down the eight stages of the twin flame relationship.

After you've completed this section, you will have all the keys to understanding what twin flames are and how to define the twin flame relationship. This is important to understand before you start diving into the methodology to prove it.

Chapter 1
Twin Flame History

There are many stages, developments, awakenings, ups, downs, and sideways to every twin flame relationship. All of these are based on what your soul needs to learn to evolve. The most important thing to understand about twin flames is that there is only one other soul in the entirety of God's creations that can possibly be your twin. You may hear this concept referred to not only as twin flames, but also "twin souls," "twin rays," or "other half." It is all the same and refers to the other half of your soul. There is another concept that closely aligns with twin flames and it is about soul mates.

A soul mate is not the same thing as a twin flame. In the Souliverse (which is what I call the universe of souls that surrounds us), you can have thousands of soul mates. Their purpose is to help you progress on your journey of soul evolution and to allow you to assist them with theirs. Soul evolution involves learning lessons and gaining knowledge to grow physically, spiritually, mentally, and emotionally. Soul mates are designed to assist. This is contrary to your twin flame, whose presence in your life often creates chaos due to the powerful energy that is at the core of the relationship. Basically, soul mates help you learn, but your twin flame instigates change.

Before I dive into some of the terminology that you will read about in this book, I want to talk a little bit about the Other Side. This refers to the energetic plane upon which souls exist who have departed from their physical lives. It is also referred to as "Summerland," "heaven," or "beyond," among other names, and your understanding of this plane of existence is based upon your belief in the afterlife. The word *plane* refers to a different level of energy. We currently exist on the Earth plane. Spirits exist on the Other Side, which is a higher plane of vibration that doesn't require a physical body to exist.

Think about a window for a moment. On one side of the window is Earth, and the opposite side of the window represents the Other Side. Both are separated by a thin curtain called a veil. When a human wants to communicate with a soul, or spirit, as they're most often called, they would simply draw back the curtain.

As a medium, those I work with when doing spirit communication (also called mediumship) exist on the Other Side. I will reference the Other Side (as well as mediumship/spirit communication) often, so it is important to explain them. Spirit communication, or mediumship, is simply communication between a sentient being and a spirit's soul or energy. We will discuss these in a bit more detail, but for now let's focus on twin flames.

Twin Flame Terminology

There are several terms that will be repeatedly used within this book, so it is important to understand them right from the start. Let's break them down one by one.

Spiritual DNA

For a moment, let's compare twin flames to identical twins who are born on Earth at the same time. These identical twins came from the same egg, which split in two and are equal parts of one whole. They have the same exact DNA because they came from the same place.

This is also true for twin flames. They originate from the same soul, which then is divided into two individual souls. Spiritual DNA is composed of energy from God, and it is the core of the soul. This divine core represents their oneness, so spiritual DNA is comprised of both masculine and feminine energy, which represents the universal duality, as well as a combination of higher vibrational energy that comes from the source of all that is. This spiritual DNA is only equal between twin flames, and it creates the divine connection between them on a soul level. This connection to one another will never sever, no matter what happens. It is divine and it cannot be removed. Soul mates, and others in our Souliverse, will have spiritual DNA that is compatible with ours, but it will not be equal.

Divine Masculine and Divine Feminine

The energies of divine masculine and divine feminine exist within spiritual DNA and they are shared by your divine match. The separate parts of one soul are often referred to as divine masculine and divine feminine. These monikers are incorrect. One soul is not inherently masculine and the other feminine.

This energy already exists within the spiritual DNA that is at the core of the soul. When twin flames are created, they are not split apart as masculine and feminine to create balance. These two souls are equal in every single way. They cannot contain only half of the divine source that created them within each soul. Divine masculine and feminine energies exist equally within both souls. This is the true reflection of the divine source within each soul.

While we're on this topic, it is important to remember that divine masculine and divine feminine are only on a soul level. They do not dictate the gender identification (or nonidentification) into which twin flames can incarnate. Regardless of how the twins identify on Earth, the soul will recognize its match in the spiritual DNA. The energy feels the same and it helps to draw the twins closer together. In other words, the twin flame relationship is not limited, there are no boundaries. Your twin will vibe with who you are, regardless of how you identify, or even if you choose not to gender identify.

Soul Blueprint

Since twin flames come from the same soul source, their soul blueprint is also equal. A soul blueprint is the design our soul created at its inception that holds information about which lessons to learn, which energies are needed to learn them, and all the ins and outs of how all of this is to be accomplished. It is divinely inspired by God.

For twin flames, the same lessons and energies exist. Often the approach to learning varies, depending mostly upon life circumstances, but there are no deviations when it comes to what the twins wish to accomplish on their path to soul evolution, which is the purpose of the twin flame relationship.

You're both working to evolve your souls to grow and learn. Once born into a life, the twin flames' soul blueprint becomes the guideline to how they live in that life, and the blueprint's information is stored in and accessed from the soul.

Soul Evolution

Soul evolution is an important phrase because it is the point of the entire twin flame relationship. The definition boils down to one simple idea: action that perpetuates education for the soul. Your soul already knows what it wants to learn and how it would best like to achieve those lessons. This information is stored in your soul blueprint and can be accessed at any given point in time.

You are not a human body having a spiritual experience. You are a divine soul housed in a human body having a human experience. Every single time you learn something new or try something new, no matter what it is, it is an action that educates the soul. When the soul becomes educated, it has evolved.

I know what you may be thinking, though. "Soul evolution? I thought the purpose was love!" Love is involved, yes. The soul recognizes itself in your twin flame, and the love is automatic. There is no other choice. The purpose of the relationship, however, isn't love, it's soul evolution.

You have not incarnated into this lifetime as only half of a soul. Your soul is complete as it is, and you are complete as you are, just as your twin is as well. The point of the twin flame relationship is not to complete one another, though the feeling of being complete upon meeting each other will often occur. The point is to educate the soul through experience and learning to evolve to higher levels of consciousness. Twins share their experiences and information with others as part of the evolution process. That's why you'll find so much information about twin flames. Twins have an eagerness to share their experiences being in a state of pure divinity. That is the state you are in when you encounter your twin flame.

Vibration

The term vibration refers to the quick movements of energy going back and forth or up and down or around and about a certain point. This vibration could be random or have a distinct pattern. For twin flames, the point that vibration centers around is the divine DNA in the soul. Divine DNA has its own specific pattern of movement that is unequaled anywhere else other than in its divine match.

This is entirely because you and your twin flame are the same on a soul level. You have the same divinity within you, the same spiritual DNA, and that cannot be replicated in anyone else. Because of its divinity, the twin flame vibration is extremely high. It is deeper, faster, and more profound than any other vibration you will experience. When you encounter your twin flame, your soul will know its partner by the vibration. It can't be helped because this vibration is equal.

Lightworker

This term is used most often to describe souls who incarnate on Earth to assist others, whether it is through spirituality or other methods. Often, lightworkers are referred to as "Earth angels" because their assistance can come when it is most needed by another. For twin flames, the word *lightworker* describes the action of assisting or aiding others on Earth by the sharing of themselves, their experiences, and their lessons.

They assist others on Earth by raising the vibration of the collective consciousness with knowledge and divine love.

Twin Flame Arguments

There are many arguments for, against, and about twin flames. It's important to understand that, while every single soul who has ever been created has a twin flame, not everyone really shares the same understanding of the concept. I have encountered several different arguments in my research, and I thought I would include some of them here and break them down.

1. *Twin flames and soul mates are the same thing:* Absolutely not true. You can have many soul mates that enter your life at different points to help you in various ways on your journey. You only have one twin flame.

2. *I will always meet my twin in this lifetime:* "Always" is a very subjective word. It is more realistic to say that you will meet your twin in some way, whether they are on the Earth plane or not.

3. *This whole "twin flame" thing is about the balance within the self. There is no one else involved:* The self is a singular unit, and singular units usually require another unit for balance. The entire point of the twin flame relationship is soul evolution, which begins within the self. The relationship will completely revolutionize both halves of the soul. There is no other choice. The interesting part is that, while both halves are equal, they are also independently complete. You cannot evolve only half a soul. That's like

trying to pour water into a bucket with a hole in the bottom. These are simply two souls with the same spiritual DNA and soul blueprint.

4. *The twin flame experience is between an individual's soul and higher-self:* The higher-self, which is the part of us that is connected to both the physical body and the soul, is most definitely involved. It isn't the only thing involved. The twin flame relationship is on a soul level. The soul learns and evolves. You cannot be in the relationship and not evolve in some way. It simply defies the very definition and purpose of twin flames. The higher-self is a part of this process because one cannot evolve without gaining a higher understanding of themselves.

5. *Twin flames are the opposites of each other. That's where the phrase "opposites attract" comes from:* Twin flames have the exact same spiritual DNA and soul blueprint. They have the same goals, the same desires, and the same lessons to learn. Granted, sometimes they can achieve this education in vastly different ways. Twins are the same at their core. They are not the same person, of course, but their actions, thoughts, words, goals, desires, and experiences will be similar and parallel. They cannot help it.

6. *An animal cannot be your twin flame:* Most often, animals (including pets) are soul mates rather than twin flames. However, this does not mean that one or both twins cannot incarnate into an existence as an animal. The twins' goal of soul evolution may require that one or both twins incarnate as an animal to further educate the soul. For example,

the twins could incarnate as lion and lioness, or a mother cat and the runt of her litter. Another possibility is that one soul could incarnate as human and its soul match could incarnate into an existence as a domesticated animal. Then of course, that presents the possibility that animal could be adopted by their twin flame. The bottom line when it comes to twin flames is that anything is possible.

How to Know When You've Met Your Twin Flame

The twin flame relationship is the purest love you will feel because at the core of the soul is divine love. It isn't necessarily romantic love, unless that is the way you've contracted with one another to educate your souls. It goes far beyond any definition of love our minds can assign and our hearts have felt.

You feel an instantaneous connection, as though you have been walking in darkness and suddenly someone flipped on a light. (This is when your soul recognizes its vibrational match!) You have the sense that you have known this person your entire life. You have a curiosity about them, and a desire to be near them at all costs. A feeling of completeness also overcomes you, and at times this feeling can be overwhelming. These feelings are unlike any other feeling or emotion that you have ever experienced before because you are literally meeting the other part of yourself, your match, your divine partner. This is the soul that God created just for you.

This is a list of the common indicators of the twin flame relationship. The more items that can be identified and understood on this list, the greater the chance of proving the twin flame relationship.

- Instant bond and connection that is unlike anything else you've ever experienced.
- You understand one another when others cannot.
- Telepathy.
- Similar or compatible birthdates.
- Overwhelming feeling of unconditional love, even if it doesn't make sense and regardless of the length of time you've known one another (a.k.a. "love at first sight").
- Explosive chemistry.
- Meeting (often at a young age), separating, reuniting.
- This person appears in your dreams prior to and after meeting them. They have also had dreams about you.
- Recurring numbers (11:11, 444, 333, 777) that center around this person you've met.
- Feeling as though you've always known one another.
- Shared/common belief system.
- Shared/common points of view.
- Shared/common/complementary strengths in character.
- The background stories of both people have similarities, possibly even "coincidences" where both of you experienced something similar at relatively the same time.
- Meeting this person gives you a renewed and deep sense of purpose.
- Meeting this person perpetuates a spiritual awakening.
- Meeting through unusual, unplanned, or unexpected circumstances.

- Deep feelings about and an awareness of the sacred connection or oneness that was previously either unexperienced or unknown to you.
- The pair are inseparable, always connected to one another in various ways.
- The desire to be fully open to each other and to your shared experiences within your relationship.
- Realization of the twin flame purpose on Earth, which is helping humanity.
- Self-realization of your soul's purpose.
- Self-realization of your spiritual path.
- The fulfilment and resolution of all karma.
- Intimacy and friendship on all levels is unparalleled and unlike anything else ever experienced.
- Creates a desire to learn more, not only about this other person but also yourself.
- Creates a complete upheaval in your life.
- You feel a sense of completion in that you have met your soul's divine match.
- You feel a mutual sense of respect for one another.
- To look at, touch, or be around with this person is completely natural, no matter how long you've known one another.
- Feeling completely fulfilled in your relationship. There is nothing lacking.
- Unconditional love and understanding of one another. Miscommunications are minimal without outside interference.

One of the amazing things about the twin flame relationship is that it doesn't have to be difficult. Yes, things will likely completely change or feel turned upside down, inside out, and backward. Just simply recognize that and understand that both of you are here for the same purpose.

The plain truth is that whether you ever meet one another on Earth or not, your twin flame walks a parallel path to yours; both of you have similar lessons to learn and both of you will feel love and loss. If you are blessed enough to meet your twin on Earth, hopefully you can work with one another to get through those times when things feel topsy-turvy.

Genealogy and Ancestry

Genealogy is the study of the line of continuous descent between ancestors. Ancestry is the study of your ancestors using ethnicity. If twin flames incarnate on Earth at the same time, they will often do so with several commonalities in their ancestral and/or genealogical backgrounds. This can range from ethnicity to common names on their family trees. In some instances, the twin flames could even be related in their current existence on Earth. They could both have German ancestry, for example, or both could have grown up in similar surroundings.

Since twin flames are equal, several commonalities will exist in both twins' ancestral and genealogical backgrounds in their current existence. If one twin has either already transitioned or did not incarnate, then of course the similarities would be found in their previous existence. There are so many possibilities here that the proof seems as though it would be endless.

Twins could have the following in common: ancestry, birthplaces (including countries, states, cities, and circumstances of birth, such as both being born outside of a hospital), shared names in family trees, both were raised in similar surroundings (city, country life, or moved around a lot), both have a similar family life (divorce, parents still together, multiple siblings, or an only child), name changes, similarities in personality, common hobbies or interests.

If there are similarities in ancestry, it is possible that there might be commonalities in appearance. If there are true, genuine similarities in the appearances of both twins, those will be immediately evident and undeniable. For example, Chico and I are similar in height, have the same natural hair color, wear the same shoe size, and have other similarities in appearance. These similarities exist thanks in part to both the spiritual DNA and soul blueprint that we share.

This list is not all-encompassing, but it does give you a start of things to consider when it comes to your twin flame. Twins will always incarnate with discoverable connections across the board.

Chapter 2
Types of Twin Flames

There are two types of twin flames: incarnate and discarnate. To *incarnate* or be *incarnated* means that a soul has chosen to be born into a life. Incarnate twin flames are souls that are born into an existence at the same time. The word *discarnate* means that the soul is without a physical form. This means that one of the twins is on the Other Side. This can happen when one of the twins chooses not to incarnate and stays on the Other Side to assist their twin on Earth. It can also happen when one twin exits their physical existence and transitions to the Other Side.

There is a lot more focus on incarnate twin flames. This is because the desire to find and meet one's twin is often overwhelming and powerful. No one really wants to think about the possibility of not meeting their twin flame in a physical existence, especially if you believe that the twin flame relationship is the ultimate love affair and all others pale in comparison. It is true that the bond between twin flames is incredibly deep and intimate, and it cannot be compared with any other relationship. This divine relationship is on a soul level with the exact match of your soul, which is why the twin flame relationship will be and feel different that any other you have previously experienced. This relationship turns everything on its head, allows it to implode into chaos, and then puts it back together from the soul outward. This evolution is the soul's truest expression. However, the possibility of discarnate twins should not be ruled out just because they lack physicality. The connection between twin flames exists no matter what plane either twin is on. The close bond between twins is there regardless of whether one of them has a body.

My initial research lacked information about discarnate twin flames outside of my own experience. It was through meeting other twins on Earth and sharing in their journeys that I learned the most common form of the twin flame relationship involves a separation of the twins between planes of existence. The twin on the Other Side assists their partner on Earth. Lessons are still learned, and soul evolution is still achieved. This is not to say that incarnate twins do not exist, especially on Earth. They do.

There are many more twin flames choosing to incarnate on Earth at the same time than ever before. They may not be aware of one another, and they may not have met, but they have both incarnated to learn and to help educate others. This is mostly because there is a huge shift and rise in the collective consciousness that has opened doors for twin flames to come to Earth to learn, to ask questions, and to try and come together.

There is renewed curiosity in concepts like twin flames. More people are tuning in to the idea, for example, that it is possible to truly communicate with those on the Other Side. When we shift our personal consciousness and raise our vibrations to open our mind to different ideas, concepts, and possibilities, the world around us shifts accordingly. This is because we are all interconnected to each other. I refer to this as the spiritual domino effect.

This effect is most represented by the fact that so many spiritual practitioners in nearly every genre of modality, from healing to mediumship, are more commonplace now. Twenty years ago, you might have found one talk show that had a few episodes with a psychic medium as a guest. Now, there are a handful of television shows specifically about mediumship, and and even more shows that explore paranormal and metaphysical topics, such as ghost hunting. This is the result of the higher collective vibration, which twin flames have contributed to simply by sharing knowledge based on the lessons they've learned.

Currently, you can find hundreds of websites and podcasts online about twin flames. This was not the case when my research began. The spiritual dominoes still spill over every single day and it is in this higher vibration that more twin flames are being born and united.

Incarnate Twin Flames

Recall that the word *incarnate* means to physically exist. This occurs when both twin flames are housed in their own physical body and experience life. Usually twins incarnate into lives on Earth because Earth is the "school" planet where souls come to learn many lessons over the course of several lifetimes. It is possible that twins have also chosen to go to another planet in some other solar system in a distant galaxy. Perhaps their lessons were best learned in an existence elsewhere. They are, however, still incarnate, even if they may not be with their divine match on Earth.

Having both souls incarnate on Earth doesn't happen as often as one may think, despite the rise in the collective vibration. It is a rare privilege to meet and be in a lasting relationship with your twin flame on Earth. This is because the relationship is a journey with the purpose to educate and evolve the soul. Some folks may not understand that calling and that is often because one twin is ready for the ups and downs of the journey and the other is not.

This is not to say that you cannot meet and be involved with your twin here on Earth. You absolutely can. Usually, when twins meet on Earth, it is because they're both ready to move forward on the journey together. They have learned all they can without meeting their counterparts, and they need their twin to continue. Also, sometimes twin flames just plain want to be together no matter what. They are willing to work through the extreme highs and lows of the twin flame relationship together, which isn't a bad thing. It's usually out of chaos that the best lessons are learned.

Before I mention our next sets of twin flames, it's important to understand that, while these twins came together and lived in physical union, they were not without struggle. The twin flame relationship is about soul evolution, so when twins come together, there can be situations where it seems like gas is added to a fire. Regardless of the struggles, however, there is the soul bond that guides them through. That bond is founded by the divine spiritual DNA at the core of their souls.

There are ups and downs in every relationship, no matter what the connection. The intensity of the roller coaster ride within the twin flame relationship is unequaled. This is because it occurs on a soul level. It should also be noted that the entire twin flame vibration is higher than your natural vibration, which can often make coming together feel very strange at first. However, nothing worthwhile is ever easy.

Zenda and Carl

There is another set of twin flames that I'd like to introduce you to: Zenda and Carl. Their experience on Earth speaks to the roller-coaster relationship that occurs with twin flames. They met in June 1972 when Zenda got a summer job at the same fiberglass manufacturing plant that Carl worked at. They were both young and had only known each other four months when they decided to get married. Zenda and Carl were married in October 1972. They just knew they were meant to be together.

Within a few months of their wedding, however, several misunderstandings, as well as third-party interference, caused a rift between the two of them that could not be repaired, despite their longing to be together. Nothing they tried worked. They separated and eventually divorced. Zenda was pregnant with their child at the time.

Both went on to marry other people and have more children, but neither were happy with their lives and they longed for one another. Both carried mementos and tokens with them every day that reminded them of one another. In late 1990, Carl's divorce from his second wife became final. Zenda decided to reach out because she believed that her daughter had a right to know her father. On the day his divorce papers came in the mail, Carl was able to speak with his daughter for the first time in both of their lives. It was a struggle for Zenda because this new communication reignited her soul, but she also had a family. After much soul-searching, she filed for divorce from her second husband. A year later, Zenda and

Carl were reunited and remarried after a separation of almost eighteen years. They were together until Carl's passing in July 2015. Their road was not smooth and never ceased to be a roller coaster, which demonstrated how they chose to learn and evolve, both separately and together.

Emily and Bobby

Another example of incarnate twin flames is Emily and Bobby. They didn't meet under the best circumstances. Emily had just broken up with one of Bobby's friends and was on a night out, unable to drive home. Emily called Bobby for a ride home, and the next morning he showed up at her door with coffee. He was still in a long-term relationship when he and Emily formed a close friendship that eventually developed into more.

Once Emily discovered that he was still in a relationship with another woman, she tried to end things with Bobby, but she couldn't. She was already in love with him, and it was difficult for her to go against her principles and stay with him. Eventually, Bobby decided to end his long-term relationship and he and Emily are now married. However, this did not happen without a lot of trials and tribulations.

Emily describes their relationship this way: "It was a catastrophe. Our relationship was so passionate yet so volatile. ... It took time to show him what love was and for him to accept it, acknowledge it, and give it back." It was a work of love that is still in progress, and the more they grow and learn from one another, the more educated their souls become.

We will discuss these couples more in future chapters, but it was important to introduce them to you now. When discussing incarnate twin flames, it is important to remember that it is a difficult journey when you're together in any kind of relationship. These two relationships are perfect examples of the ever-changing roller-coaster energy that exists within the twin flame vibration.

Discarnate Twin Flames

The word *discarnate* means that the soul has no physical presence. In other words, the discarnate twin has no body. This is because they have either transitioned from their physical existence to the Other Side, or they remained on the Other Side to assist their twin flame on Earth. Though we were both incarnate on Earth simultaneously for twenty years, Chico and I fall into this category. He passed away several years ago and has been by my side from that moment, even if I didn't realize that it was him or why he was there.

During my research, I was most interested in reading information about how to communicate with your twin flame if they aren't on Earth. Such information wasn't in abundant supply when I first started researching. The opportunity to directly communicate with the other half of my soul would, it seemed to me, mean that we could become closer.

If we'd tried this on Earth in the physical, there could have been so many other inhibitors. For example, would we be each other's "type" of partner in a romantic relationship on Earth? I'm not sure Chico necessarily had a "type" of girl, but I do know that he wouldn't have fallen into my category of guys I crushed on. These limiting beliefs would likely have impeded any communication on Earth as well as possible opportunities I may have had to meet him when he was on Earth. There is no such thing as "types" on the Other Side. It is all about the soul, which is always a perfect match for twin flames, regardless of physical appearances on Earth. There is no reason at all for twins to have any lack of communication or connection.

Often, the easiest way to achieve soul evolution is by having one twin incarnate on Earth and the other twin on the Other Side, looking at the soul blueprint to help guide their counterpart. Your souls are always in constant contact, even if your conscious mind has no clue who your twin is. We will cover this more in the metaphysics sections, but there are ways to communicate with your discarnate twin flame without necessarily being a medium.

I know of twins who communicate with each other through song titles. For example, I know of a pair of twins where one twin is here on Earth and the other has been on the Other Side for many years. The twin on Earth simply asks for specific song titles from his twin on the Other Side and inevitably his request is granted every single day. I also know twins who use forms of divination, such as pendulums and spirit boards, to communicate with their partner on the Other Side. This is a concept we will discuss in detail later in the book, but I mention it here merely to illustrate other possibilities. Still, there are other twins I know who communicate with each other by utilizing a medium to assist them. You always have the option to directly communicate with your twin, you just need to see the possibilities.

Twins on the Other Side only have one limitation when it comes to their twins on Earth. The conscious mind is very quick to shut out, block, or dismiss things it doesn't truly comprehend or make it frightened in any way. So those on the Other Side can try and try to get through, but if their counterparts on Earth can't or won't listen, then that is a limitation that inhibits the twin flame relationship.

Jesse and Andy

I'd like to introduce you to another set of twin flames, Jesse and Andy. Though these two people had several mutual friends and they lived and worked in the same town, they missed several opportunities to meet one another. Jesse was a reporter who covered the local entertainment scene and Andy was heavily involved in the theatre scene. Jesse had written several reviews about various plays and musicals of which Andy was a part, but there was never any reason for Jesse to interview him specifically. Their mutual friends were convinced that the two of them should meet and the phrase "two peas in a pod" was often used in their circle to describe Jesse and Andy. Finally, after many failed attempts at getting these two together, their first date was all set up, with a mutual friend, Aaron, spearheading the entire event.

It was Aaron who also called Jesse two days before the date and broke the news about Andy's sudden passing. In that moment, Jesse became overwhelmed and emotional. His body shook from head to toe, and he began to cry so hard he became physically ill. Aaron couldn't understand this reaction, after all, Andy was his friend, not Jesse's.

Days after, Jesse called Aaron again, and explained that he was in the middle of an emotional breakdown over Andy's death. He didn't understand why this was happening at all. Neither Aaron or Andy could find a rational reason that made sense to them, so they both decided to consult me, both as a friend and as a professional psychic medium.

During our session, Andy gave me the privilege of being his voice so he could communicate with both Aaron and Jesse. Several months had gone by since Andy's passing, and he told us that he discovered that he and Jesse had a unique connection: they were twin flames. Since I was also still knee-deep in learning about this concept at this time, I recommended that Aaron and Jesse consult other mediums simply for validation. Over the course of about six years, nine other mediums—none of whom knew anything about Aaron, Jesse, or Andy—validated this connection.

Even though his reaction made no sense at the time, Jesse discovered that the reason he became so emotional was because his soul knew what his brain did not: its equal and partner had departed from the physical life. His soul grieved this physical connection on Earth.

Jesse spent the rest of his life until his death researching the concept of twin flames and the twin flame relationship, including assisting me in my own research. He was able to further his understanding of his own relationship through our shared research. And he eventually gained the understanding that the entire reason he began to write theater and entertainment reviews was because Andy had drawn him close via their soul connection. Neither one of them started out as writer or actor, respectively. Yet it fascinated Jesse (and Aaron and their friends) at just how close they came to one another.

You must remember that the twin flame relationship is on a soul level. You are literally two halves (although they are complete halves) of one whole soul. The soul grieves for the loss of the physical life. Think of your reaction to a family member's physical death. You grieve for them. And while grief is a personal process for everyone, your grief comes from your soul.

It was important to introduce you to Jesse and Andy now because their story indicates that the process of finding your twin, discovering your connection, and creating a relationship never ends, even after physical death. It also doesn't matter if both twins are on Earth or separated by the veil between Earth and the Other Side. Twins are always connected. Not even physical death can change that.

False Twin Flames

A false twin flame is someone that you believe fits the definition of your twin but is not. You can believe for years that you have found your twin, but they do not actually share any of your spiritual DNA nor do they have the exact same soul blueprint. Often, we search so long and so hard for our twin flame that when we find our ideal partner, we instantly believe they must be our twin.

False twin flames are soul mates in disguise. On occasion, a soul mate enters your life, and they embody almost everything you could ever believe your twin flame could possess. You'll notice that I used the word *almost*. This is because there is something missing from the false twin flame relationship. It could be a lack of things in common or feeling unfulfilled or constantly having disagreements. There is nothing lacking in a valid twin flame relationship.

The surefire way to recognize a false twin is straightforward: a false twin does not create positive change in your life that perpetuates soul evolution. This is difficult to realize while you are in the middle of the relationship, but it is unmistakable. A false twin does not create positive change in your life that perpetuates soul evolution. These changes apply to both twins, not just one.

If drama, argument, pain, hurt, or anything like that is all that exists in your relationship and it occurs without positive resolution and without both of you learning anything, then you aren't with your twin. The entire purpose of the twin flame relationship is soul evolution, pushing one another to learn and grow and develop. If this doesn't happen, then no matter what you may feel or believe, you aren't with your twin.

Real twin flame relationships aren't designed to hurt or cause either twin to be in pain or misery. There will be ups and downs, just like in every relationship, but the goal is to help each other learn. Abusive relationships, for example, cannot be a valid twin flame relationship. This can be any type of abuse: verbal, physical, sexual, narcissistic, or emotional. There is no room in the twin flame relationship for this energy.

You must remember that twin flames are the same in their soul. They have the same goals, ideas, thoughts, personalities, wants, needs, desires. If you are in a relationship with someone you believe is your twin flame, and if you have cause to question this connection at all, then there is likely something missing. You may want to reevaluate your connection and relationship.

Chapter 3
Roles and Stages

Before we dive in, it's important to reiterate the fact that you are not a human having a spiritual experience. You are a soul made up of divine energy that is housed in a physical presence made of flesh, blood, and bone. Your soul is having a human experience to grow, learn, and evolve itself.

This complex human body in which our souls exist contains a complicated consciousness. It also is made up of energy, from the smallest strain of DNA to the outer layer of skin on your entire body. It's all energy, and energy retains information.

The energy in our bodies reacts to the energies around us, from the people in our environment to the chair we sit in. Everything consists of energetic grids that vibrate at different frequencies. The only other energy that matches yours exactly is your twin flame. This is because you have the same spiritual DNA.

When twins come together, no matter if they are incarnate or discarnate, any energy that you carry with you, such as pain, hurt, emotional baggage, fear, shame, anger, or hatred, all automatically come to the surface. This is because it needs to be cleared out to continue to evolve and grow. The soul cannot evolve if it is mired in or covered up with these lower vibrational energies. These energies cannot coexist with the powerful and extremely high vibration of the divine love that exists at the core of your soul. Since there is no other energy in the entirety of creation that exactly matches yours, there is no one better than your twin flame to assist you with getting rid of this lower energy that no longer serves your best and highest interests.

The issue is that when twins come together and this massive energetic release occurs, they have no clue what's going on and why. As a result, the process that's designed to draw the twins closer to one another does the exact opposite, and this creates roles of "runner" and "chaser" that exist within the twin flame relationship.

The good thing is that it really doesn't have to be difficult. It always sounds difficult, especially when it comes to roles and stages and everything they entail. But, if you open yourself up to fully experiencing everything that occurs in this relationship, then life gets a little easier.

Runner and Chaser

The runner is the twin who cannot handle the intensity of any or all parts of the twin flame relationship. They withdraw from their twin completely, which causes more pain because the natural inclination for twin flames is to draw closer to one another, not the opposite. There are times when the intensity could make both partners just want to head for the hills.

Running is triggered by this massive energy release that automatically begins when twin flames meet one another. This energy release is comprised mostly of negative energy, so there will be triggers. Remember, energy retains information, as does your soul. There is an energetic footprint of everything that occurred in your life within your aura and in your soul, and these can be difficult to revisit and release. Often, the twin flame relationship gets the blame for these triggers and thus one twin rejects their counterpart. If there is a pattern of rejection within this energy release, the twin may see this relationship as just a setup for another failure. They have no idea that this isn't possible. You can't fail to create a relationship with your twin flame. It's been there since your souls were created.

The chaser is the twin who is the peacekeeper in the relationship. This is because the chaser instinctively knows that everything will turn out just fine once the current crisis is over. The chaser is often aware of the fact that the runner is afraid of letting go of what is normal and familiar to them, which is the result of this massive energy clearing that occurs between the twins. They realize that this energy is built up of fear and that the largest fear is rejection. This twin is going through the same exact things and often is inclined to run away, but they do not.

True twin flames will return to one another, there isn't another choice. They are divinely connected. And it is the chaser who most often continues to work on the relationship. Anything one of the twins does to work toward soul evolution will also affect their counterpart. This means that if you are a chaser and you decide to sit and meditate every day or seek out ways to assist with clearing out all that old energy, this will impact both twins. Releasing this energy raises your vibration, and your twin will also experience a higher vibration.

By keeping the peace within the relationship, the chaser can energetically assist the runner in letting go of the energy that triggered them to run away from the relationship. Once the runner returns, the twins' collective work continues.

Stages

Everywhere you read about twin flames, you will find not only runner/chaser information but also information about the stages of the twin flame relationship, of which there are several. These stages occur no matter on what plane or planet the twins are located. Love never ends, no matter what happens between the twins. These stages are a roadmap to soul evolution.

Don't expect to reach every single stage in one lifetime. Often, it will take several tries to evolve the souls. Conversely, sometimes your souls have already worked for eons through many lifetimes to achieve the energetic clearing that takes place during the initial stages. In the present incarnation, that could mean that the twins might move through these stages a little bit faster.

Here are the stages as I understand them and have experienced them. I believe there are eight stages, as eight is the number of infinity and twin flames are eternal.

Stage One: Recognition and Awakening

Though the twins' souls instantaneously recognize and know each other, their conscious minds do not have a clue. Meeting and recognizing your twin flame triggers an awakening, not just of the twin, but also of the self. I liken it to going through the queue at an amusement park. You know you're about to get on the roller coaster, but you truly have no idea what to expect until you experience it firsthand.

The awakening is triggered by the souls' deep desire to move forward toward soul evolution. And, once triggered, the twins begin to merge energetically, often through chakra alignment. This is essential as what one twin experiences, so does the other.

The key to working through this stage is trust. Trust yourself and your feelings. Most importantly, trust that your soul recognizes its exact match. There can be no error when true twin flames meet one another.

Stage Two: Ascension

You are seated in the car of the roller coaster, belted in, and the car is moving. This stage is the stage where everything begins to turn upside down and inside out. Connection with your twin will bring about an energetic process that will bring to the surface everything that has been pushed down and buried deep within you. All this energy comes to the surface so that it can be dealt with, learned from, and let go. This prepares you for the twin flame union.

The key to working through this stage is to relax. You are experiencing the emotions and feelings that trauma left behind. Make the conscious decision to release all of this and allow yourself to do so. You will have your twin right by your side, and it also helps to know that they are going through the exact same thing you are.

Stage Three: Learning and Evolution

You are in the car on the roller coaster as it goes up and down, looping, turning upside down and twisting. This is the stage where everything is laid bare and you are deep in the energetic flow of your emotions. If you have triggers or buttons that cause any kind of upset, they will come out. You can also discover and uncover that you may have triggers that stem from trauma in past lives. This happens with amazing intensity, due to the fear of everything that rises to the surface.

Fear completely governs this stage, so it is important to remember: Feel Everything and Release (F.E.A.R.). Learning becomes part of the releasing process because you can learn from your experience and become educated about yourself. You can learn exactly why certain situations still trigger you, for example.

The key to working through this stage is to remember that, while fear is totally in charge here, it is easier to go with the flow than to resist. The tendency here is to push things to the side or ignore events or circumstances that caused a significant amount of pain. Pushing them aside won't do you any good, they will come back to the forefront with a vengeance.

Stage Four: Running

I liken this stage to getting sick while on the roller coaster. The entire contents of your stomach spill out and there is no stopping it. This stage cannot happen without the learning and evolution stage. Everything comes to the surface, and it is during this stage that one of the twins decides to run. It is far too painful to continue any further. There are deep feelings of anger, defiance, judgment, and resistance, among others, as well as an incredibly horrible fear of rejection. Both twins can experience these feelings during the process, as there is much to release and learn and fear.

The key to making it through this stage is simply to understand that by getting rid of all this stuff that has been held in for so long, it clears out stale and stagnant energy. Doing this allows the twins to become energetically and often physically closer to each other. This is the genesis of actively working together toward soul evolution.

Stage Five: Surrender

You step off the roller coaster. You may be a little worse for wear, but you made it to the end, and it was, overall, an incredible experience.

Here, surrender doesn't mean to "give up." Rather, it means that you can let go of the pain and fear to see more positivity enter the relationship. The more negativity released in stage three, the more energetic space there is in this stage to bring in higher vibrations such as joy, peace, and love.

The twins are no longer fighting or bogged down in negativity. Rather, a natural positive flow opens between them and their relationship changes to one that is absent of fear. The twins are attracted to one another energetically, like a magnet to metal, instead of wanting to run away or chase one another. Also, neither twin is afraid of rejection anymore. They both realize they are in this forever.

The key to working through this stage is to trust and believe, no matter what anyone else may say or do. You and your twin are an unbreakable team. Believe it.

Stage Six: Challenge

As if the twins need another challenge, right? In this case, it doesn't mean that there is another hard or difficult mountain to climb. Rather, it means that the twins will push each other beyond their limits and help one another to think outside the box—all with love—to achieve their goals.

Often during this stage, the twins will separate from one another to find their footing in their own lives. This is not the same as running away from the relationship. Rather, this is a conscious decision both twins make to ensure that they are on the right track in their personal lives. It doesn't necessarily denote a physical separation; it could be that both twins take a break from lesson learning with one another. True twin flames are never apart, they are always divinely connected.

When the twins return to each other, they do so with the intention of standing beside one another on their journey forever. There is no more "I" or "you" in this stage. It is "us" and "we."

The key to navigating this stage is to remember that the work you do for yourself will always energetically translate to your twin too. You are polishing the diamond that is your soul.

Stage Seven: Illumination and Merging

The twin flame energetic merging begins in stage one. It is part of the awakening. In this stage, however, the merging goes beyond the chakras and includes blending of energies. This blending cannot fully occur until each twin's energy is clear enough so as not to damage their systems by this merging. Sometimes, especially if one twin is on the Other Side, this is the stage where twins could pick up each other's habits or speech patterns. There may be previously unknown common physical characteristics that come to the surface as well. Do you know the adage, "The longer we're together, the more we're alike"? It usually speaks to couples who have been together for decades. It is an example of how twin flames can physically express the equality and sameness of their souls.

It's also during this stage that telepathy and the ability to connect with each other in absolutely every possible way increases exponentially. Often, at this stage, the twins are so connected that they can access each other's memories, feelings, and thoughts, or even finish each other's sentences.

In this stage, the twins experience another, more powerful awakening. This awakening does not contain the triggers, buttons, or fears that the previous one did. Rather, this is an awakening to each other that can only be defined as illuminating. It is in this awakening that you experience, see, feel, and know everything possible about your twin flame. There's no holding back. Everything is laid open for one another to experience.

For those whose twin is discarnate, this stage could happen concurrently to all others. This is because you have the capacity to communicate directly with one another without any kind of impediment or Earthly limiting beliefs. It's also likely that you can receive dream communication, or also your twin's memories while you're in dream state. There isn't a need to "access" them because they can be freely given. Often, there will be a lot of similarities in these shared communications. These commonalities will be less of a surprise now and more of a confirmation.

I think it's safe to say that this stage hasn't stopped for me and Chico. We learn something more about one another every single day. The more we learn, grow, and understand one another, the closer we become and the more our energies blend.

The key to functioning in this stage is to allow; allow whatever comes and accept it as fact. At this point in your relationship, there are no barriers between yourself and your twin. There's no reason to have any, no reason to keep secrets or to hold back any kind of emotions or experiences. It is all a part of the shared journey.

Stage Eight: Union

In this stage, the twins have let go of ego and fear and are energetically unified in unconditional love. They are no longer separate and function as one. They can now work as lightworkers, spreading the message of love to the planet.

Also, in union the twins can move quicker toward soul evolution. The lessons are learned and knowledge gained quickly, often with lightning speed. There is no time to worry about fears or any of the lower vibrational energies. The union has created a singular body of light and it can function only from the highest universal vibration: pure love.

Don't misunderstand, there will always be lessons that need to be learned. But in union, you have learned everything necessary and let go of what is equally unnecessary to be a fully functional partner in the twin flame relationship. Also, your thoughts, words, and actions all become one because you are aligned with your purpose.

Chico and I won't really say that we're "in union," which is the fashionable thing to say in the twin flame community. The belief is that once you have located your twin, you automatically go through all the stages and then you are in perfect "union."

We are of the opinion that a true lightworker's work is never done. To assist others, we must be willing to grow, learn, and evolve, which means that there are always going to be new things to learn. We learn them as one because we are energetically unified. We will never stop learning. What you are reading now is the result of our energetic union.

The thing about union is that it exists from the inception of the soul. Twins are always connected and are always one. The rest of the stages serve to assist twins in becoming closer to one another and clearing the energetic path toward soul evolution. In each stage there are lessons. Each of these lessons educates the soul.

Part 2
The "-ology" Methods

In this section, we begin our discussion of the various methods used to prove the twin flame relationship. We will begin with methods that have existed for millennia: numerology and astrology.

We already know that the purpose of the relationship is soul evolution. The purpose for proving the twin flame relationship is similar. Learning about the divine counterpart perpetuates change and growth. For each method, there are lessons that will assist you either with gaining an understanding or enhancing the knowledge you already have. Every single calculation you complete will educate your brain and your soul, thus helping to assist in soul evolution. The more you learn and grow, the closer you become to your twin. These methods put this divine connection in the spotlight.

A true and valid connection will show itself. These methods simply help to bring this validation to the forefront. In many ways, the methods discussed within this book have been used for eons in connection with several topics, including twin flames. We have purposely made these methods simple to help others utilize them. The methods we describe may not be the way you use or are familiar with astrology and numerology. We have created new ways of utilizing them to further our understanding about twin flames. Each method in this book will assist you on your journey with your twin.

A word of advice: if you are in the early stages of a friendship, a new romantic relationship, or anything similar, please don't start asking for birth information to prove the twin flame relationship. If you start asking what time someone was born on the first date, that can be awkward. If you believe you've met your twin flame, allow yourself time to get to know this person before you start in on processing these methods. You just may discover that everything flows so naturally that you don't even have to ask the first question.

At the conclusion of this section, you will be able to create your own (and your twin flame's) numerological and astrological charts. You will also have several more pieces to the twin flame relationship puzzle in the form of data divined from these charts.

Chapter 4

Numerology

Numerology is the study of the numeric value of things within your life. This can be in words, names, or even concepts. Numerology also examines the correlation between specific events and numbers. The operational theory of this method is that twin flames incarnate with similarities that can be numerically calculated. These similarities can be found in almost everything involved in each of their lives, from the smallest thing (like a driver's license), to life paths or birth (and death) dates.

There are several facets of numerology we'll discuss in relation to twin flames. Before we begin, we must list the twin flame numbers. These numbers numerically define the energies that exist within the twin flame relationship, so it is important to understand them.

Twin Flame Numbers

One is called the oneness number. This is because it indicates energetic and soul oneness, not just between all souls but specifically between twin flames. The oneness number may also symbolize new beginnings, new energy, and new growth. For twin flames on their journey of soul evolution, this meaning is quite important. There is always the opportunity for new energy to enter into the twins' lives that will open doors to further educate the soul. The oneness number holds space for both twins to be open to this new energy.

Seven is the universal number because it symbolizes the infinite and divine connection to the universe. For twin flames, this number also symbolizes the divine connection between souls. It's a symbolic number for twins because the horizontal line at the top of the numeral creates the connection between two souls and the vertical/diagonal part of the number indicates the oneness of both souls. This number is important to twin flames not only because of its symbolism, but also because this universal connection will assist soul recognition when the twins meet, no matter what plane they're located on.

Eight is known as the infinity number because it symbolizes divinity and eternity. In its regular, upright numeric form, this number forms a divine figure eight of energy, which is the energetic flow that runs between the universe and the soul, thus creating a constant connection. For twin flames, the number eight in its numeric form represents the journey of the self that begins when twins unite. The twin flame relationship is designed to be an internal journey first to work on the self. This internal work will also prepare you for the journey toward soul evolution with your twin flame. It's a given and natural part of the twin flame relationship.

The number eight turned on its side signifies an even deeper meaning for twin flames. This is called the infinity symbol, and it signifies the unbreakable and eternal bond between twin flames. The number eight also indicates significant or major change within your life. Meeting and working with your twin flame, regardless of what plane they're on, is major on a life-changing level.

Now, we begin with the master twin flame numbers. These numbers are called master numbers because their natural energy is amplified at a higher vibration than a single digit. Their energies also hold space to create healing and manifestation within the twin flame relationship.

The master number eleven is the most recognized of all the numbers related to twin flames. I refer to this number simply as the twin flame master number. Most often, this master number is seen in the form of 11:11, which is usually a sign that you have encountered your twin flame. The master number written in this form signifies that the amplified energies of both twins are joined. Recall our discussion about the divine masculine and divine feminine. When the soul is split into two, each half has both these divine energies within its DNA. When we give this energy numeric value, each soul is represented by an eleven. If a soul encounters their divine match, the numbers and energy would be the same. Therefore, the numeric representation of the meeting of twin flames is 11:11. In addition, if you think of 11:11 as bookends to the energy that flows between them, then you can see why the number eleven is also called the Pillar of Twin Flames.

The number twenty-two is the master builder number. It is the double of the number eleven and indicates the energetic buildup of lessons for soul evolution. These lessons usually run parallel, regardless of whether the twins know one another at the time. It is also very often the case that these parallel occurrences will bring twins closer together, as they're basically learning the same lesson at the same time. Think about it this way: if the number eleven represents one soul, and 1+1=2, then the master number twenty-two is a visual representation of the parallel alignment of both twins.

Finally, the number thirty-three is the master teacher number. This number indicates a desire to teach the knowledge twins have gained. The reason it is so is because any variation of this number, 3, 33, 333, 3333, and so on, indicates you have become self-empowered, not only within the twin flame relationship but also within yourself.

This master number is also associated with higher realms, such as the angelic realms and the ascended masters. For example, Jesus, Buddha, Confucius, Mother Mary, and Saint Germain are a few of the ascended masters. Such energetic empowerment opens up both twins to working with the higher realms on the other side, with the goal of sharing any knowledge that's gained.

Using the Numerological Method

To prove the relationship using numerological calculations, the following must be present: repetitive numbers, twin flame master numbers, calculations that can be divided by two or whose final calculation is equal to two, exact same numbers, or calculations with resolutions equal to a number on the Fibonacci sequence.

These calculations and their results are present to demonstrate the energetic similarities of twin flames. Twins will have repetitive numbers and master numbers that show up even in the smallest calculation. Also, typically if twins are going to incarnate together in the same lifetime, their birthdays will have the element of eleven in them or a division of two between them. The number two is the single digit breakdown of the master number eleven and therefore it's used to divide.

You will notice that if you add up the individual numbers within the master numbers twenty-two and thirty-three, these numbers can be divided by two:

22: 2+2=4 (divisible by and equal to two)

33: 3+3=6 (divisible by two)

The twin flame number eight can also be divided by two. When you add the other two twin flame numbers (one and seven) together, it is equal to eight. Two is a popular number in this method.

We will also discuss twin flame numerology and break down numerological charts. This method applies to these charts in the same way. It's all about commonalities in the results of calculations, and they can show up anywhere, no matter what you choose to calculate.

Creating Your Own Calculations

In this section we discuss how to create your own calculations. We will also reference master numbers, repeating (or repetitive) numbers, and calculations that involve and/or result in the number two. It's important to remember that the presence of these numbers in abundance indicates the energetic connection of twin flames. It is your first piece of the twin flame relationship puzzle.

You should start easy when it comes to calculations. Start with what you know. If you know the birthdate of your twin, all you need to do is write it out numerically and add it up until you get to a single digit. For example, say you want to figure out December 31, 1970. You would write it like this: 12-31-1970. Then you would add up the individual numbers like this: 1+2+3+1+9+7+0. This equals twenty-four; two and four added together equals six.

The number six is divisible by two, so there you would have your first piece of the numerological puzzle. Honestly, don't be like me and just start adding everything you find right off the bat. When you first begin, try with birthdays, and then maybe move to anniversary dates, dates of significant events, or special times.

Twin flames will always have commonalities and similarities. It doesn't automatically mean that your birthdays will both add up to the same number. In fact, you'll soon see that this really isn't usually the case. However, this initial calculation can show whether you're on the right track. Remember, you're looking for any of these in your calculations: repetitive numbers, twin flame numbers and master numbers, division of or equal to the number two, mirrored or equal numbers.

The idea is to look for common threads, starting with birthdates, to prove mathematically not just that you're compatible, but also that you are twins. Twin flames will not incarnate into a lifetime without a way to calculate, map, divine or prove the relationship. That would be counterproductive to the purpose of soul evolution. If you've reached a point where you are truly interested in learning about and proving the relationship, then you will find the means, methods, and evidence to prove it beyond the shadow of a doubt.

It also helps that calculations can be done on anything. I have pages and pages full of calculations for all types of things from license plates to shoe size, to the distance between our birthplaces. It's easiest to start off with simple things, like your birthdates. No matter what the calculations are, be sure to record them and save them. All the information will eventually come in handy.

Sample Calculations

Twins usually have important dates in their relationship where numbers repeat, have a master number present, or are the same number. This is regardless of what types of numbers you factor in (birthdays, birth times, driver's license numbers, social security numbers, etc.). Here are some examples from the calculations for me and Chico:

There are 1,109 days between his birthday and mine. If you add each number together, it equals eleven, which is a master number. One would need to write out the complete date, using the numeric equivalent of the month and full year, to properly complete this calculation. Then you would calculate it to a single digit. This calculation eventually adds up to the number two, which fits in with the theory discussed earlier. Let's go on to another calculation.

One of the most important dates in our relationship was the date he entered my dreams and said, "Hello." That date was June 6, 2006. One would need to write out the complete date, including year, to properly complete this calculation.

As you can see, the calculation eventually adds up to the number two, which fits in with the theory discussed earlier. Let's go on to another calculation.

Our birthdates and times and Chico's passing date and pronounced time of death are also important. If the twin flame relationship is proven on Earth, it is proven period, no matter what plane the twins are on. The best way to help prove the relationship on Earth is by using birthdates, birth times, and even a death date if your twin is discarnate. The birth times for myself and Chico add up to six , for example. The death date and time can be used in the calculations because the two mark the final moment the soul was on Earth. A true and valid twin flame relationship can be proven right up until the souls' final moments on Earth. Play around with these dates and numbers. The relationship will reveal itself in commonalities.

Chico's birthdate and time = 9

Chico's death date and pronounced death time = 7

My birthdate and time = 6

Now add these numbers together:

9+7+6=22 (master number)

2+2=4

The number four can be divided by two, and the result of that calculation is equal to two.

Here, our shared time on Earth is calculated and broken down to the number four, which is divisible by the popular number two. So, it does indicate an energetic connection. The more calculations you do, however, the more it becomes evident that it's not just a connection. It's your twin flame.

Let's do this calculation again using only the calculations from my birthdate and his death date, just so you can see that no matter what numbers you use to compare, similarities will be found.

6+7=13

1+3=4

The number four can be divided by two, and the result of that calculation is equal to two.

Think of some more examples of calculations. They can be done on anything. The more comparative calculations you do the better.

The distance between the cities in which we were born is equal to 2,016 miles and the shortest driving route takes thirty hours. My calculation adds all this information together:

2+0+1+6=9

3+0=3

3+9=12

1+2=3 (repeating number)

Let's do a couple of calculations for our other twin flame couples. You will be able to see that there are endless possibilities when it comes to what you can add, subtract, multiply or divide.

Jesse and Andy

Andy's birthdate and time = 1

Andy's death date and time = 7

Jesse's birthdate and time = 2

Jesse's death date and time = 1

Now add these numbers together:

1+7+2+1=11 (master number)

1+1=2

There are 6,735 days between their birthdays.

6+7+3+5=21

2+1=3

Andy's driver's license number added up to two, Jesse's added up to nine.

2+9=11 (master number)

1+1=2

The distance between their birthplaces is 165 miles, and the shortest driving route takes three hours.

1+6+5=12

1+2=3

3+3=6

This number can be divided by two, and the result is equal to the number two.

Just in these three examples, we see the master number eleven is one of their repeating numbers. I have completed several calculations for them, and I can say that eleven, three, five, six, and nine are numbers that are consistently repeated.

Zenda and Carl

Carl's birthdate and time = 4

Carl's death date and pronounced death time = 8

Zenda's birthdate and time = 4

You'll notice that both of their birthdates add up to the same number of four. This is just one of the many commonalities that can be an indicator of the twin flame relationship. The more similarities you calculate the better. Now, add these numbers together:

4+8+4=16

1+6=7 (universal number)

There are 1,408 days between birth days.

1+4+0+8=13

1+3=4

This number can be divided by two, and the result is equal to the number two.

An interesting thing about Zenda and Carl is that they were married twice. Let's break down their wedding dates.

First wedding: 10-14-1972

1+0+1+4+1+9+7+2=25

2+5=7

Second wedding: 10-14-1991

1+0+1+4+1+9+9+1=26

2+6=8

Nineteen years between weddings = 1

Now add these numbers together:

7+8+1=16

1+6=7 (universal number)

In these calculations alone, the universal number seven repeats within the results. Other repeating numbers include four, five, and the infinity number eight.

Emily and Bobby

Emily's birthdate and time = 9

Bobby's birthdate and time = 4

It's noteworthy that Emily and Bobby were born in the same year, and that their birthdays are eight months apart (eight is the infinity number). Now, let's add these numbers together.

9+4=13

1+3=4

This number can be divided by two, and the result is equal to the number two.

There are 228 days between birth days.

2+2+8=12

1+2=3

If you take this three from the result of the calculation of days between their birth, and add eight months to it, the result equals a master number:

3+8=11 (master number)

1+1=2

This was just an extra, fun little calculation to do, but it really does factor in when it comes to repeating numbers. Let's look at one more calculation with Emily and Bobby. Their wedding date is July 28, 2018.

7+2+8+2+0+1+8=28

2+8=10

1+0=1

The number one is a twin flame number, and it is also a repeated number throughout all the calculations I've completed. The other repeating numbers are three and four.

The reasoning behind this methodology insists that twin flames will have similarities and commonalities within every aspect of their existence, and these can be calculated. The twin flame relationship is evident when you find results that are repeated numbers, equal numbers, master numbers, or numbers that can be divided by the number two. Keep in mind that this is one piece of the overall puzzle, but at least it's a corner piece that's easily recognizable.

The Fibonacci Sequence

The Fibonacci sequence is a mathematical sequence associated with divine pattern and twin flames. The sequence follows the pattern of 0, 1, 1, 2, 3, 5, 8, 13, 21, 34, 55... and so on.

It is the golden ratio that is reflected in things such as sacred architecture, octaves in music, roses, pinecones, or spiral seashells. It is an illustration designed to show the oneness of our divinity and how we are all interconnected through a divine pattern. The sequence is calculated by adding up the two numbers prior, starting with zero. Written as a mathematical rule, the expression looks like this[1]: $x_n = x_{n-1} + x_{n-2}$. You will immediately notice that the twin flame number one and the ever-present number two exist within the mathemat-

1. Tia Ghose, "What is the Fibonacci Sequence?" LiveScience, last updated October 24, 2018, https://www.livescience.com/37470-fibonacci-sequence.html.

ical expression of the sequence. This is another reason why these numbers are used in the twin flame calculations.

The sequence is the universal pattern of nature, a numeric footprint for the foundations of sacred geometry, which is the divine natural creations we experience such as roses and pinecones. Sacred geometry defines the patterns of the universe (think of spirals, circles, triangles, squares, and rectangles). Without it, things like tables, boxes, and pyramids cannot be defined.

The sequence is also present in our physical DNA, displayed as a spiraling (sacred geometry) double helix with measurements of 34 angstroms long by 21 angstroms wide.[2] When you add the measurements of the double helix together, the result is the number one. This is yet another indicator of the divine connection, and it's within the cells of the body's physical makeup. It serves as a perfect example of how intimately both the physical and spiritual bodies work together.

When it comes to twin flames, the sequence embodies the mathematic representation of the twin flame relationship. On one hand, the sequence begins with zero, or a complete soul, and then is followed by the number once twice, which indicates the equal souls. On the other hand, the sequence begins with the master number eleven, which is why this number is the highest vibration of all master numbers. Also, as previously discussed, the number eleven is the mathematical representation of one soul.

If the sequence began another way, then the entire concept of sacred geometry would be forever altered. The same is true

....
2. George Dvorsky, "Fifteen Uncanny Examples of the Golden Ratio in Nature," Gizmodo, last updated February 20, 2013, https://io9.gizmodo .com/15-uncanny-examples-of-the-golden-ratio-in-nature-5985588.

with twin flames. This explains the concept that if the souls are not equal, you cannot be twin flames. It goes against the natural and mathematical symmetry and inclination. Think of it this way: if an orange is cut in half, both halves are equal. They have the same design and the same number of slices you can peel off and eat. It's sacred geometry. You cannot slice an orange in half and have one part looking like an orange and the other part looking like an apple. It just isn't possible and the sequence proves that.

Pythagoras, 11:11, and the Fibonacci Sequence

We already know that the number 11:11 is associated with twin flames. This repeated number is a numeric representation of two souls meeting. It is also based on the ones found in the Fibonacci sequence. These numbers are called the Pillar of Twin Flames. When you consistently see 11:11 repeating, it is usually a sign that you have encountered the energy of your divine match.

The origin of this belief is rooted in the discoveries of Pythagoras. He based his revelations on musical theory, in which notes could be worked out in proportions that included 2:1 (octave), 3:2 (perfect fifth) and 4:3 (perfect fourth). This is relative to the golden rule and the Fibonacci sequence. The octave, fifth, and fourth form the base for musical scales and intervals.

Let's briefly discuss a bit of musical theory. The vibration of perfect harmony is written as 1:1. (This shouldn't be surprising when you think of twin flames as being in perfect harmony with one another.) An octave, 2:1, means that something is vibrating twice as much. For example, Pythagoras discovered that plucking a string that was half the size of another will create a pitch that is exactly an octave higher. Also, plucking a string that is twice the size of another will sound an octave lower.

An octave is the collection of eight tones or vibrations. If you play through the C major scale (Do, Re, Me, Fa, So, La, Ti, Do), by the time you get to the high C you have completed one octave. If you split a string into thirds, then you raise the pitch an entire octave and a fifth. Split it into fourths and the pitch goes even higher. This forms the basis of the perfect fifth and perfect fourth, which can be mathematically calculated along with octaves using different formulas. In short, the working theory for Pythagoras was that everything, including music, could be better explained and defined through mathematical calculations.

Pythagoras also theorized that all parts of the universe, including planets, sounded out specific notes based on their distance to one another and the planets' orbits. These notes could be translated not only into numerals but also mathematical calculations. He then applied this theory to explain that numbers had their own vibration and these numbers helped to create harmony and balance, or 1:1. His numeric table and definitions worked like this:

- The number one represented oneness and the origin of everything.
- The number two represented women.
- The number three represented men.
- The number four represented justice.

- The number ten represented perfection because
  $1+2+3+4=10$.[3]

Pythagoras determined that everything began with the sacred number one. Then, as the vibrations continued, they would develop into what he called the "holy four," which were the numbers one, two, three, and four. These first four digits add up to ten, which is the number of perfection.[4]

You'll recall during our brief discussion about the master number eleven that when a soul is divided into two equal halves, both halves contain divine masculine and divine feminine energy. Each energy is represented by the number one, which is how one half of the soul is mathematically represented by the number eleven. Pythagoras' theory was that everything begins with the number one, which represents oneness. There is validation for one of the digits that represent the soul. Validation for the other is this: Pythagoras believed that everything adds up to the number ten, which is the number of perfection. If we break that number down to a single digit, we get the other one that represents the soul. This theory proves that the soul is numerically represented by the number eleven. Since the numbers within this mathematical theory add up to eleven for only one soul, and both souls must be considered, this is where the other eleven comes into play. Two equal souls is represented by 11:11.

....

3. Encyclopedia Britannica, "Pythagoreanism," accessed February 2020, www.britannica.com/topic/number-symbolism/Pythagoreanism.
4. Colin Wilson, *The Occult: A History* (New York: Random House, 1971), 209–211.

This mathematical representation of twin flames is also found in a similar way on the Fibonacci sequence. Here's a reminder of the sequence: 0, 1, 1, 2, 3, 5, 8, 13, 21, 34, 55 ...

It begins with zero, and then includes two ones. These ones are thought to represent twin flames because each number one is a soul. However, one soul is mathematically represented by the number eleven, not the number one. So, to use the sequence to mathematically represent and define twin flames, we must use it twice. It can be broken down this way: zero represents the complete soul and the two ones that follow represent the divine masculine and divine feminine that exists within the soul, which would also be eleven. If you did this calculation twice, you would end up with the 11:11, which is the true Pillar of Twin Flames.

The energy in the Fibonacci sequence is closely tied to birthdates and birth names, similar to astrology. These calculations for the sequence are a precursor to working out specific parts of the numerology chart.

During your calculations, you will find that a lot of the results will be numbers that are on the Fibonacci sequence. If only your numbers match the sequence and not your possible twin flame, then this is not proof of the twin flame relationship. Both twins must have calculations that result in numbers that match the sequence. This is because it signifies oneness and divine pattern, as well as sacred geometry—all of which are used, in one form or another, to illustrate and illuminate the twin flame relationship.

So, take a moment and retrieve the calculations you have done so far for yourself and your divine match. Make sure they are broken down to a single digit, and then compare them to the sequence. You will find that a lot of the numbers will correlate.

Life Path Numbers

You will read more about life path numbers when we break down the numerological charts in the next section. But I wanted to give a section specifically to life path numbers because by themselves, separate from the charts, they can be used to help prove the twin flame relationship.

A life path number is considered the most important numeral in a numerology reading. It's calculated by adding up all the digits in a birthdate and simplifying the numbers down to a single digit. A life path number represents all the situations you attract because of your knowledge and actions. A life path number's energy will stay with you throughout your entire life because it is based on your birthdate. Though you can go through various cycles that can be calculated using the current date and your birthday, the life path number you were born with doesn't change. Its energy helps shape your life.

This number is generally a number designed to assist you in your self-work on your spiritual journey. The more work you do, the closer you come to being prepared to begin walking the path with your twin. When it comes to the twin flame relationship, this number is a strong indicator of the overall life lesson that you incarnated to learn according to the soul blueprint. Since this soul blueprint is shared between twin flames, it should be equal or compatible.

The basic meanings of the life path numbers are below. Keep in mind that there is much more to them and they're worthy of research. However, for the purpose of proving the twin flame relationship, the basic meanings will do. These meanings can also be applied to other numbers within the numerological chart.

- Life path number one will have the characteristics of a natural born leader.
- Life path number two will have the personality of peacemakers (and often a peacekeeper).
- Life path number three signifies those who are motivators as well as those who are in communications or some other form of self-expression.
- Life path number four is for those who are students, teachers, and love to learn. There is also the ability to create order and achievement within this life path number.
- Life path number five symbolizes adventurers and doers, as well as action and freedom to go and do what one wants to do.
- Life path number six is for those who are natural nurturers, counselors, those who have a parental and responsible side to their personality.
- Life path number seven is for spiritual seekers, psychics, and those who have an individuality that doesn't conform to the normal ways of society.
- Life path number eight is for those who gravitate toward becoming business leaders or who are excellent in manifesting what they want and need in their lives.
- Life path number nine will be compassionate humanitarians.
- Life path number eleven is associated with those who are highly psychic and intuitive. They will also have peacemaking capabilities like those in life path number

two. Illumination (or enlightenment) and magic will also play a huge part in their personalities.

- Life path number twenty-two will have the characteristics of those who love to learn or who are master builders and visionaries.
- Life path number thirty-three is associated with master teachers, creativity, those who are informative, and natural nurturers.

Twin flames incarnate with either equal or complementary life paths. The numbers themselves can be equal, both even, both odd, divisible by each other, or divisible by the number two. Twins will not incarnate with life path numbers that have meanings that do not either match or complement one another.

To find the number, add up all the digits in the date of birth and simplify them down to a single digit. If you come across any of the twin flame master numbers in your calculations, take notice of them because therein lies additional validation.

- My life path number is seven (spiritual seeker).
- Chico's life path number was three (communicator).

We are natural born leaders who, using our individual traits, share the information that we learn with others. In other words, what I seek, he communicates and vice versa. You can see how these individual life paths are complementary and work together to achieve the goal of soul evolution.

Let's break down the life path numbers for our other twin flame couples.

Jesse and Andy

Jesse's birthday is February 4, 1950.

2+4+1+9+5+0=21

2+1=3

Jesse's life path number is three (communicator, motivator).

Andy's birthday is August 29, 1958.

8+2+9+1+9+5+8=42

4+2=6

Andy's life path number is six (responsible, counselor, nurtures).

It takes motivation to communicate with others. It also takes a nurturer to be responsible and counsel others. Together the two create an environment of compassion for humans.

Zenda and Carl

Zenda's birthday is December 12, 1954.

1+2+1+2+1+9+5+4=25

2+5=7

Zenda's life path number is seven (spiritual seeker).

Carl's birthday is February 4, 1951.

2+4+1+9+5+1=22

2+2=4

Carl's life path number is four (student, learning, teacher).

It is by seeking, especially spiritually, that we learn. Being a student who is constantly learning allows one to teach others what they've learned.

Emily and Bobby

Emily's birthday is April 22, 1985.

4+2+2+1+9+8+5=31

3+1=4

Emily's life path number is four (student, learning, teacher). Bobby's birthday is December 5, 1985.

1+2+5+1+9+8+5=31

3+1=4

Bobby's life path number is four (student, learning, teacher).

Life path numbers must be equal or compatible to prove the twin flame relationship. Here they are equal. The student can manifest what is important (and sometimes what is desired too), thanks to their education. Often, this is indicative of excellent business skills and knowledge. It just comes naturally.

Discarnate Twins and Numerology

I used the information for several discarnate twins in all the calculations so far. Remember, Chico, Carl, Andy, and Jesse have all passed from their Earthly existences. A few notes about discarnate twins: If both twins incarnate into a lifetime at the same time, then of course there is no trouble using this information at all. If one twin passes from their life, leaving the other on Earth, the energy of their numerology chart ends the moment they pass. The information used to calculate both the astrological and numerological information comes from their most recent incarnation on Earth, no matter if that was six months ago or one hundred years ago.

A soul on the Other Side has no need for a life path number or a rising sign. Both the numerological and astrological charts are like a snapshot in time when both twin flames were incarnate on Earth. This methodology is a tangible and mathematical way to prove the twin flame relationship on Earth. Twins cannot be born into an existence anywhere, whether it's on Earth, Mars, Pluto, or in some other far-off galaxy, and be someone else's twin flame. Twins are a team from the moment of soul creation.

In short, it doesn't matter if your twin is on the Other Side or on another planet. There is a point in time that exists within the history of your souls where you both were human on Earth. Information from that moment is what is used to conclusively prove the twin flame relationship.

Twins cannot incarnate and be incompatible, so if you do not know anything about your discarnate twin's most recent life, you can ascertain some information by using your own. If I use the example of my life path number without the benefit of knowing Chico's life path number, I understand that my twin would be someone who may be a student or a person who perhaps had means to communicate knowledge. Students are also seekers of knowledge. And because I am a spiritual seeker, my twin could not be anything less than the same. As it turns out, Chico was indeed a communicator and a seeker of knowledge. He stood up for those who could not speak for themselves, and he shared his knowledge with countless others.

Remember: twin flames are always connected to one another. You are never separated, not even when only one of you is on Earth.

There will always be an opportunity to learn about your twin. It is inevitable because, regardless of what plane your twin is on, they're going to want you to know about themselves. This is usually when you can discover more about them during things like pastlife regression or an Akashic Records reading. From these sessions, you can discover information about your twin's last existence and possibly calculate both the numerological and astrological charts accordingly.

Regardless, you must remember the basic fact that your twin will not incarnate and be opposite of you or incompatible with you in any way. You will likely share many beliefs and experiences, and will also likely surround yourselves with the same kind of people (whose souls are part of your Souliverse). So, even if you have zero specifics about your twin, you must know that they are your equal on a soul level.

Creating Numerology Charts

There is an entire chart that can be created from birth information and various parts of given birth names. I learned how to build one of these charts from the ground up. The longer I worked on this, the more astonished I became at how much more the twin flame relationship was evident within the chart.

Each letter is assigned a numeric value. It isn't exactly one through twenty-six though, because remember double digits are reduced to singular ones. For this methodology, we look again to Pythagoras.

While there are other tables used in numerological calculations, the vast majority prefer the Pythagorean Numerology Table. In this table, there are nine columns, and you start with the letter A in the first column. You keep filling in the table with letters beneath numbers until you have reached the letter Z.

Pythagorean Numerology Table

1	2	3	4	5	6	7	8	9
A	B	C	D	E	F	G	H	I
J	K	L	M	N	O	P	Q	R
S	T	U	V	W	X	Y	Z	

The theory for proving the relationship doesn't change when it comes to the numerology chart. You still need to look for common numbers, twin flame numbers, repeating numbers, and exact numbers. The chart lays these numbers out for you. It also opens the door to deeper understanding of not just how the two of you are twin flames, but also how your relationship is defined.

The more of these numbers that you configure, the more things can become clearer to you. Start by using your own name and birthdate to calculate your numerological chart. Once you have completed yours, you can then calculate your twin's. The following breaks down the basic meaning of each number and how to calculate it. Each number is also explained in twin flame-ese to better understand how these numbers relate to the twin flame relationship.

- *Life Path (Birth Force) Number:* Contains all your accumulated wisdom. Your life path number never changes and stays with you throughout your life. To calculate your life path number simply add up your full date of birth, including all four numbers of your birth year, and reduce to a single digit. For twin flames, this is an indicator of the overall life lesson you incarnated to learn. It should be equal or compatible because this lesson comes from the shared soul blueprint.

- *Birth Number:* This number helps you to better understand the important lessons to be learned and how your innate abilities can assist. To calculate your birth number, add up just the digits of the day you were born. If you were born on the twenty-fifth of the month, for example, you would do the calculation like this: 2+5=7. For twin flames, this number indicates the lessons, both individually and collectively, that you've chosen to learn. These should be equal or compatible numbers, as the lessons are always the same.

- *All Letters Number:* This is the energy of your birth name in numeric form. This can also be used for compatibility purposes. To calculate this number, add up the numeric equivalent of all the letters of your first, middle, and last name (surname) using the number values of each letter per the Pythagorean Numerology Table. For twins, breaking down your names to single digits allows you to see both individual and collective energy between you. You will also see your overall compatibility. Remember, twins cannot incarnate incompatible. It just isn't possible when twin flames have the exact same spiritual DNA and soul blueprint.

- *Heart's Desire (Soul Urge) Number:* This number connects you with what is most dear to your heart, as well as your innermost desires. It directs your purpose and successes. To calculate your heart's desire number (often also called the soul urge number), add up the value of the vowels *a, e, i, o,* and *u* in your first, middle, and last name using the numeric values of each letter according to the Pythagorean Numerology Table. The letter *y* counts as a vowel if there are no other vowels in the name. For example, if someone's name includes the word "yellow," the *y* would not be a vowel because of the *e* and *o*. For twin flames, this number should be equal or compatible because it comes from the shared soul blueprint. Compatibility is indicated here when calculations between the number either equal two or can be divided by two. You both know what you want and how to get it, and a lot of the time you want the same things. You just go about achieving them a little differently.

- *Personality Number:* This number represents how the outside world views us at first impression and how these views affect us. To calculate your personality number, add up the value of the consonants in your first, middle, and last name using the numeric values within the Pythagorean Numerology Table. The letter *y* would count as a consonant here if there are vowels present in the name. Again, these should be very similar, if not equal, numbers for twins. If the personalities are vastly different here, then you have not located your twin flame. Twins will not incarnate with opposite personalities.

- *Expression (Destiny) Number:* This number indicates your life and soul purpose. It has two names used interchangeably, expression and destiny, but for our purposes we will stick with expression. To calculate this number, add your heart's desire and personality number together and reduce to a single digit. Since this number represents purpose, compatibility and similarity is essential in this number for both twins. This number added together for both twins indicates the overall life purpose that could be accomplished within the twin flame relationship.

- *First Consonant:* This number provides insight to how you deal with the outer world. This number is the numeric equivalent of the first consonant in your first name. This numeric value is found in the Pythagorean Numerology Table. This number has to do with how we deal with the outside world. For twins, this would simply indicate similarities. This could be on a soul level, too, but more likely it is how each twin reacts to the physical world.

- *First Vowel:* This number provides insight to how you react to your spiritual world. This number is the numeric equivalent of the first vowel in your first name. This numeric value is located on the Pythagorean Numerology Table. This number relates to the spiritual and nonmaterial world. For twins, there really must be compatibility here because it has less to do with the physical and more to do with the spiritual. Twins connect on so many levels, including the spiritual level. This number would indicate how each twin processes their journey in the spiritual and non-material (nonphysical) world.

- *Growth Number:* This number provides insight that assists us with growth and development. To calculate, use the Pythagorean Numerology Table to assist you and add up the value of the letters of only your first name.

- *Point of Security (Habit Challenge) Number:* This identifies patterns that are repeated by which we feel challenged. To calculate, count the total number of letters in your first, middle. and last name. For example, Leslie has a total of six letters, therefore I would use six to represent my first name in this calculation. Once you have counted these numbers, add them together and reduce to a single digit. For twin flames, there will likely be similar or equal patterns and actions. This is because, though each twin will have learned behaviors and responses, their actions and responses will likely be similar.

• *Maturity Number:* This number represents how you will outwardly express yourself to find happiness, opportunities, and satisfaction later in your life. This number is the sum of your life path number and your expression number. The focus here for twin flames is a sense of knowing how well each twin achieved each individual and collective goal and lesson. This indicates where the twins are at in soul evolution. The closer, more compatible these two numbers are, the more achieved.

• *Personal Year Number:* This is your overall current vibration. To calculate, add up your birth month, day of birth, and the universal year number (see next page) and reduce to a single digit. Calculating this number is important to understand what you should accomplish (or not accomplish) this year. The meanings for each number are below. For twins, this indicates both individual and collective goals for the year. These should either be equal or compatible when looking at the individual numbers.

1. Embrace the energy of new beginnings.
2. Have patience for the things for which you have planted seeds.
3. Expression and creativity open new doors for you.
4. Take the time to get organized in all aspects of your life.

5. Reap the benefits of the seeds planted.

6. Focus on relationships with others, as well as with yourself.

7. Reflect, return to nature, take a break, and look within to gain.

8. Out of reflection and hard work, now is the time to manifest.

9. Let go of the old, complete the cycles you haven't yet finished.

- *Universal Year Number:* This describes the general planetary vibration of the current year. To calculate, add up the four digits of the current year and reduce to a single digit. For twin flames, it numerically represents one year of the soul blueprint. The meanings for the universal year number are the same as those for the personal year number.

- *Personal Month Number:* This number represents your vibration in the present month. To calculate this number, add the numeric value of the current month and your personal year number and reduce to a single digit.

- *Personal Day Number:* This number indicates a good day for spiritual growth or self-care. To calculate, add your personal month number and the current day digit together and then reduce to a single number.

- *Personal Month and Day:* These numbers both piggyback on the energy of the personal year number, only it boils it down to the month and day. Doing so indicates, basically, what's going on that month or day. It's a smaller piece of the overall larger puzzle of your personal year. For twins, this is just another way to whittle down the energy. It is also a strong indicator of where exactly the twins are when it comes to accomplishing their individual and collective goals. If the personal year number is the destination, the personal month and day numbers are the GPS.

Numerological Chart Comparisons

Here are Chico's and my charts using our birth names. Note that the calculations were done using our full first, middle, and last names given at birth. Further note that the maturity number does not technically count for Chico since he passed to the Other Side. I calculated it anyway and included it in our chart just so our chart would be complete (and besides, it turned out to be a repeating number).

Numbers	Leslie	Chico	Total	Single Digit	Notes
Life Path	7	3	10	1	Master number
Birth	5	5	10	1	Master number
All Letters	6	8	14	5	Repeating number
Heart's Desire	5	7	12	3	Repeating number
Personality	7	1	8	8	Master number
Expression	3	8	11	2	Breakdown of master number eleven
First Consonant	3	9	12	3	Repeating number

Numbers	Leslie	Chico	Total	Single Digit	Notes
First Vowel	5	9	14	5	Repeating number
Growth	8	9	17	8	Master number
Point of Security	7	6	13	4	Divisible by and equal to two
Maturity	1	2	3	3	Repeating number
Personal Year	6	5	11	2	Breakdown of master number eleven
Personal Month	7	6	13	4	Divisible by and equal to two
Personal Day	8	7	15	6	Divisible by two and equal to repeating number.
Total				55	

There are many numbers in the single digit column that are on the Fibonacci sequence. You will also note that there are multiple master numbers, repeating numbers, and numbers divisible by two that are evident in the overall combination of our charts. Now, let's take the total for the single digit column and break it down:

5+5=10

1+0=1

Our entire numerological charts break down to the number one. This number is also on the Fibonacci sequence and is one of our repeating numbers. It is amazing to see how all the numbers come together to paint a mathematical picture of the twin flame relationship.

Let's look at the numerology charts for our other twin flame couples. Please note that I left off the personal year, personal month, and personal day for their charts because these numbers constantly change.

Zenda and Carl

Numbers	Zenda	Carl	Total	Single Digit	Notes
Life Path	7	4	11	2	Breakdown of master number eleven
Birth	3	4	7	7	Master number
All Letters	7	6	13	4	Divisible by and equal to two, repeating number
Heart's Desire	5	8	13	4	Divisible by and equal to two, repeating number
Personality	2	8	10	1	Master number
Expression	7	7	14	5	Equal numbers, repeating number
First Consonant	8	3	11	2	Breakdown of master number eleven
First Vowel	5	3	8	8	Master number, repeating number
Growth	5	7	12	3	

Numbers	Zenda	Carl	Total	Single Digit	Notes
Point of Security	1	1	2	2	Equal numbers
Maturity	5	2	**7**	7	Master number
Total				45	

There are several numbers in the single digit column that are on the Fibonacci sequence. Again, almost every number is either a breakdown of a master number, a master number, equal numbers, or divisible by the number two. So, this would prove our operational theory. Let's break down the total number:

4+5=9

It is noteworthy that the numbers four and five are both repeating numbers for these two.

Jesse and Andy

Numbers	Jesse	Andy	Total	Single Digit	Notes
Life Path	3	6	9	9	Repeating number
Birth	4	2	6	6	Divisible by and equal to two, repeating number
All Letters	3	2	5	5	Repeating number
Heart's Desire	5	6	11	2	Breakdown of master number eleven
Personality	9	3	12	3	Repeating number

Numbers	Jesse	Andy	Total	Single Digit	Notes
Expression	5	9	14	5	Repeating number
First Consonant	3	4	7	7	Master number
First Vowel	5	9	14	5	Repeating number
Growth	8	6	14	5	Repeating number
Point of Security	3	2	5	5	Repeating number
Maturity	8	6	14	5	Repeating number
Total				57	

Again, there are several numbers here that are also on the Fibonacci sequence. You can see all the similar numbers that are represented here again. Every number is either a master number, a repeating number, or divisible by two. Let's break down the total number.

5+7=12

1+2=3

Their combined charts add up to the number three, which is compatible with their combined life number of nine. You can also divide nine by three, and that result is equal to three, which is a repeating number. The life number three is about communications, expression, and motivation, which has the energy of assisting others. The life number of nine denotes compassionate humanitarians. These complement each other very well and is one more indicator of the twin flame relationship.

Emily and Bobby

Numbers	Emily	Bobby	Total	Single Digit	Notes
Life Path	4	4	8	8	Master number, also equal numbers
Birth	4	5	9	9	
All Letters	9	8	17	8	Master number
Heart's Desire	2	3	5	5	
Personality	7	8	15	6	Divisible by and equal to two
Expression	9	2	11	2	Breakdown of master number eleven
First Consonant	4	9	13	4	Divisible by and equal to two
First Vowel	5	6	11	2	Breakdown of master number eleven
Growth	1	9	10	1	Master number
Point of Security	2	1	3	3	Repeating number
Maturity	4	6	10	1	Master number
Total				49	

As with our other couples, there are numbers represented here that are on the Fibonacci sequence. You will notice that nearly every number is either an equal number, a master number, a repeating number, or divisible by two. Again, this fits into our theory that the twin flame relationship is proven when there is an abundance of similarities within the numerology chart. Now, let's break down the total number and see what we get.

4+9=13

1+3=4

Their charts break down to the number four, which is one of their repeating numbers. It is also divisible by and equal to the number two. The life path number four represents students, teachers, learning, and achievement; which goes hand in hand with their combined life path number of eight; which is manifestation and business leaders. Another interesting fact is that you can divide their combined life path number eight by four and it is equal to the number two.

We learn quite a bit by examining our numerological charts, but the most prevalent thing when it comes to the twin flame relationship is that it breaks everything down one piece at a time. It also shows you how each piece defines the twin flame relationship.

———

You're sick of numbers and math right now, right? I know I was. You can add numbers from now until your fingers cramp up and you'll likely get an entire range of things that match up with the theory and its proof.

I have calculated everything from names to social security numbers, to driver's licenses, to phone numbers. The more you calculate, the more you will find that no matter what you add, subtract, multiply or divide, a true and valid twin flame relationship will be evident. Whether it is a twin flame number, a repeating number, an equal number, or a number that is divisible by two, it all will fall right into place.

Be sure to keep these calculations handy as, again, they are all just one more puzzle piece to the overall goal of understanding and proving the twin flame relationship.

Chapter 5
Astrology

Astrology is the divination of the influence of the planets and stars on people and events by using their positions, aspects, and symmetry.[5] The operational theory for this method is that the twin flame relationship is proved through commonalities divined from the astrological birth charts of each twin. These commonalities indicate parallel lessons that each twin is working on, as well as common threads in their life paths.

This method examines the twins' birth charts and compares them on the surface. It doesn't require diving into the deep end of the astrological pool right off the bat. True twins will have indicators in their charts that you can see right away. This method will use the birth chart to illustrate evidence of the twin flame relationship. We will look at commonalities as well as opposition.

The twin flame purpose is to achieve soul evolution, so it doesn't make sense that they would be working on opposite ends of the spectrum or against one another. Opposites may attract to one another, but twin flames aren't designed that

5. Merriam-Webster, "Astrology," accessed July 1, 2021, https://www .merriam- webster.com/dictionary/astrology.

way because they are the same on a soul level. Usually when opposites attract, it is a soul mate who enters your life to help you learn something from a different perspective.

Opposition does not negate the presence of a twin flame relationship, provided other proof exists. Rather, opposition indicates individual traits of each twin designed to assist in soul evolution. The more opposition that exists in the chart, the more progression that needs to take place. Fewer opposite traits indicate lessons have been learned and there is a greater push of progression toward soul evolution.

The Astrological Birth Chart

The astrological chart is basically a road map for a soul's time on Earth in a specific incarnation. It is an extension of the main soul blueprint that the twins share. If both twins are incarnate, then the chart can be used to determine what the soul is focused on learning while on Earth.

You can choose to do your own research about astrological charts to discover deeper meanings That is where I began my astrological journey. Chico and I have nearly the same charts, which means we incarnated with a whole lot of similarities. It is good to have a basic knowledge of the charts, because diving into them can illustrate even more similarities on many different levels.

However, it isn't necessary to understand every single nuance of your birth chart to prove the twin flame relationship. There is usually so much emphasis on studying the birth chart in as much depth as possible within the study of twin flame astrology. But, when you stop and think about the fact that the astrological chart is just a smaller version of the soul blueprint, it makes sense that one would be able to see common threads without diving too far into the birth charts.

The point when it comes to proving the twin flame relationship really isn't to study the chart deeply. Sure, you could dive head-first into the deep end of the astrological pool, but the key to proving the relationship by using these charts is on the surface. Twins have the same soul blueprint, which is the source of the astrological chart for each lifetime. The chart isn't going to hide this fact, nor is it going to make it difficult to see the relationship. The charts aren't going to require you to narrow everything down to the nearest degree. Though the twins may have elected to learn differently in their lifetimes, the goals are still the same. The charts will reflect all commonalities that exist just by looking at them.

If one twin has transitioned from their existence on Earth, then their chart for that specific lifetime is over. An infinite soul cannot be contained into a single chart once they have transcended their Earthly bodies. That soul exists throughout many facets of time and space, so it would be difficult to pinpoint a date and create a chart with any kind of accuracy. For the birth charts on Earth, you need a birthdate, birth time, and birthplace. This simply cannot be calculated from the moment of their physical death. They haven't incarnated into a new life on the Other Side. They've let go of the life they lived on Earth. Once that transition happens, the energy flow of the birth chart ends. There's nothing more to map out in that lifetime because it's over.

Because the twin flame relationship is on a soul level, the birth charts are like a snapshot of time when the soul existed in a physical form on Earth. The good news is that if you prove the twin flame relationship using astrological charts during the time these souls were living a physical existence on Earth, then it is proven, period.

Twin flames cannot incarnate into a life and be someone else's twin. You are twin flames at the creation of the soul, not at the incarnation into a new life. That cannot change, no matter on what plane or planet the twins exist.

Gathering Information

It's important to note that not all twins will incarnate with very similar charts. The birth charts for Chico and I are very similar, and we will break them down later in the chapter. Similarities indicate two things in our methodology: the twin flame relationship and lessons that have been learned.

Twins will incarnate with every indication of the relationship and their connection to one another visible in every conceivable way. One of the places that it is evident is in the astrological birth charts. If you are in a relationship with someone who you believe is your twin, you can use this method to help prove your connection. It is not the only method of proof; it is a piece within the grand puzzle. It is an important piece, and so that begs the question, "How do I get my twin's birth information?"

If you are already in a relationship with someone you believe is your twin, you may simply ask them. It is helpful to have the date, place, and time that they were born, but if they do not know the time that is fine. You can use the generic time of noon. I wouldn't ask for this information on the first date, but it is something to discuss if you are secure in a long-term relationship of any kind with the person you believe to be your twin flame.

If you are not in a position where you can receive this information, don't fret. You can still use this methodology to assist you on your way to proving the twin flame relationship. We will examine ways to determine compatibility based just on the birthdate.

Start by getting your own birth chart. You can discern from sun signs alone whether a person could be your twin. Twins wouldn't have opposition here when their entire purpose is to achieve soul evolution. Twin flames might go about accomplishing things and learning lessons using different methods, but they wouldn't work against each other.

If you do not have the information for your twin's birth chart (date, time, birthplace), then you can use the following information to rule out those who could not be your twin flame based solely on a sun sign. You can have soul mates who enter your life who have signs that are opposite of yours, but your twin cannot be opposite. You are the exact same on a soul level, and it will be evident in every measurement you research within your astrological birth charts.

Zodiac Information

The astrological signs are, in part, based on the four seasons: spring, autumn, summer, and fall. They are also partially based on the four elements of fire, earth, air, and water, and the quality determination of cardinal, fixed, and mutable. For this simple determination, however, it is common to use the exact opposites as they are found on the astrological chart.

Aries opposes Libra.
Taurus opposes Scorpio.
Gemini opposes Sagittarius.

Cancer opposes Capricorn.
Leo opposes Aquarius.
Virgo opposes Pisces.

In other words, if you are a Virgo your twin flame cannot have the sun sign of Pisces. That would make the two the exact opposite and therefore would discount the twin flame relationship.

Keep the following zodiac information handy. It lists the information about signs, houses, and planets in relation to the astrological birth chart. It also lists three aspects of astrological synastry that can help define the twin flame relationship. The chart refers to quality, polarity, and element as a means of comparing the birth charts. It is useful when determining whether signs are conjunct or in opposition. For example, an Aries has a cardinal quality, which naturally makes them inclined to initiate change. A Taurus has a fixed quality, which makes them want to preserve. They would naturally oppose one another simply based on this quality. They also oppose one another elementally (fire and earth). They do, however, balance each other out when it comes to polarity (yin/yang). That same Taurus might get along better with a Virgo, as they have a mutable quality that allows them to be flexible, the same polarity, and they are elementally equal.

- *Aries:* March 20–April 18. Aries's ruling planet is Mars and it's governed by the first house of the astrological chart. Its quality is cardinal, its element is fire, and the polarity is yang. Some keywords associated with Aries are action and new beginnings.
- *Taurus:* April 19–May 20. Taurus's ruling planet is Venus and it's governed by the second house. Its qual-

ity is fixed, its element is Earth, and the polarity is yin. Some keywords used to describe Taurus are builders and determination.

- *Gemini:* May 21–June 20. Gemini's ruling planet is Mercury, and it is governed by the third house in the astrological wheel. Its quality is mutable, its element is air, and its polarity is yang. Keywords associated with Gemini include versatile and inquisitive.

- *Cancer:* June 21–July 22. Cancer's ruling planet is the moon and it's governed by the fourth astrological house. Its quality is cardinal, its element is water, and its polarity is yin. Keywords used to describe Cancer include assertive and self-starter.

- *Leo:* July 23–August 22. Leo's ruling planet is the sun, and its governing house is number five. Leo has a fixed quality, its element is fire, and its polarity is yang. Some keywords that can be associated with Leo are forceful, generous, and impulsive.

- *Virgo:* August 23–September 22. Virgo is ruled by Mercury and governed by the energies of the sixth house. Virgo has a mutable quality, Earth is its element, and its polarity is yin. Keywords often associated with Virgo include meticulous, practical, and dependable.

- *Libra:* September 23–October 22. Libra is ruled by Venus and is governed by the seventh house. Libra has a cardinal quality, air is its element, and its polarity is yang. Keywords to describe Libra include perceptive, impartial, and intuitive.

- *Scorpio:* October 23–November 21. Pluto rules Scorpio while the eighth house is its governing energy. Its quality is fixed, water is its element, and its polarity is yin. Some keywords associated with Scorpio are intense, emotional, and loyal.

- *Sagittarius:* November 22–December 21. This sign is ruled by Jupiter and governed by the ninth house. Sagittarius has a mutable quality, an element of fire, and a polarity of yang. Keywords that can be associated with this sign are direct, honest, and truth-seekers.

- *Capricorn:* December 22–January 19. Saturn rules this sign, and it is governed by the tenth house. Capricorn has a cardinal quality, an element of Earth, and a polarity of yin. Keywords associated with Capricorn include practical, sensible, and hardworking.

- *Aquarius:* January 20–February 18. This sign is ruled by Uranus and governed by the eleventh house. It has a fixed quality, an element of air, and a polarity of yang. Keywords associated with Aquarius include revolutionary and freedom seeker.

- *Pisces:* February 19–March 19. Neptune rules this sign, and the twelfth house governs it. Pisces has a mutable quality, an element of water, and a polarity of yin. Some keywords associated with Pisces include mystical, sensitive, and loyal.

These are helpful to understand when comparing charts. Here, opposition may indicate further lessons to be learned, unless of course they occur in the sun or rising signs. We are focused on comparing the birth charts to find commonalities and similarities, which will prove the twin flame relationship. Though we will compare these on the surface, it does help to know that you can break down other aspects of astrological symmetry to locate more similarities.

We discussed the fact that there is evidence within the birth chart of lessons that have or have not been learned. It is also important to define the meanings of each planet and all twelve houses. Once you have made your birth chart comparisons, you may be interested to discover where you and your twin flame may need to explore further. It may also be interesting to note that similarities can also indicate common personality traits or shared experiences. Here's a brief overview of the houses and planets.

Planets

Sun: Symbolizes men in general; represents the essential self.

Moon: Symbolizes women in general; represents emotions, subconscious, instincts, and memory.

Mercury: Symbolizes communication style and reasoning

Venus: Represents love, beauty, attraction, and the arts.

Mars: This is the planet of desire, aggression, enterprise, and courage.

Jupiter: Represents growth, prosperity, wisdom, and abundance.

Saturn: This is the planet of organization and discipline.

Uranus: Represents inventiveness, independence, and originality.

Neptune: This is the planet of spirituality, compassion, psychic ability.

Pluto: Symbolizes renewal and transformation.

Houses

1. *House of Self:* Planets in this house influence your personality and how you are perceived by others. This house represents your rising sign.

2. *House of Money/Possessions:* This house represents your attitude toward personal wealth and how you accumulate it.

3. *House of Communication:* This house governs all communication in your environment.

4. *House of Home:* This house represents your home and is associated with the root of who you are and can affect your home life.

5. *House of Enjoyment:* This house rules affairs of the heart outside of marriage.

6. *House of Tasks:* This house governs your daily work, service, activism, and how well you perform these duties.

7. *House of Marriage:* Governs all interpersonal relationships within the bounds of marriage, including quarrels, separation, and divorce.

8. *House of Transformation & Healing:* This house is the opposite of the House of Money (second house). This house rules what a relationship owns, such as joint finances. This house also rules the processes by which we transform and become more powerful, including sex.

9. *House of Big Ideas:* This is the house of thought and ideas, and it includes our experiences when searching for the philosophical meaning of things.

10. *House of Status:* This house represents success for the sake of honor and social status.

11. *House of Community:* This house governs goals, hopes, ambitions, humanitarian interests, and self-realizations.

12. *House of the Subconscious:* This house represents our hidden self that exists separate from our everyday physical self and reality.

Comparing Birth Charts

We are looking for very simple information when it comes to the astrological birth chart. We are looking for evidence of equality or compatibility. Examples include equal or compatible sun signs, equal or compatible moon signs, equal or compatible rising signs (which is the first house), or equality/compatibility within the astrological houses.

Your combined chart should not necessarily look exactly like mine and Chico's, but the more commonalities you locate, the stronger the indication of lessons learned within the twin flame relationship. We will compare the charts between myself and Chico, as well as our other twin flame couples we discussed in chapter one.

Leslie and Chico

Here is a combination of our astrological birth charts. Keep in mind that these were only truly comparable until the time that Chico passed on. We had almost the same birth charts. Our birth information is listed below.

	Chico	**Leslie**
Birthdate:	August 23, 1970	September 5, 1973
Birthplace:	Oregon	Illinois
Birth Time:	12:03 p.m. PDT	10:43 a.m. CDT

Planet/House	Chico	Leslie	Chart Results
Sun	Virgo	Virgo	Equal
Moon	Sagittarius	Taurus	Conjunct
Mercury	Virgo	Virgo	Equal
Venus	Libra	Libra	Equal
Mars	Taurus	Leo	Conjunct
Jupiter	Aquarius	Scorpio	Conjunct
Saturn	Cancer	Taurus	Conjunct
Uranus	Libra	Libra	Equal
Neptune	Sagittarius	Scorpio	Conjunct
Pluto	Libra	Virgo	Conjunct
1	Scorpio	Scorpio	Equal
2	Sagittarius	Sagittarius	Equal
3	Capricorn	Capricorn	Equal
4	Aquarius	Aquarius	Equal
5	Pisces	Pisces	Equal
6	Aries	Aries	Equal
7	Taurus	Taurus	Equal
8	Gemini	Gemini	Equal
9	Cancer	Cancer	Equal
10	Leo	Leo	Equal
11	Virgo	Virgo	Equal
12	Libra	Libra	Equal

As you can see all our houses are equal, but only four planets are equal. This does not indicate a disproven theory, rather it overstates that we incarnated with so many similarities and commonalities that it is undeniable. The other six planets are compatible with one another on the surface of the birth chart. This is true because they are not exact opposites of one another.

Zenda and Carl

Recall from chapter one that we met a couple named Zenda and Carl. We'll also break down their charts into spreadsheet form to make it easier to see their similarities. Carl's chart was done without an exact birth time, so we will not configure the houses in our comparison between their birth charts. We are looking for equal or compatible information within their charts. Let's look. Their birth information is listed below.

	Zenda	**Carl**
Birthdate:	December 12, 1954	February 4, 1951
Birthplace:	Illinois	Kentucky
Birth Time:	12:12 a.m. CST	Unknown

Planet/House	**Zenda**	**Carl**	**Chart Results**
Sun	Sagittarius	Aquarius	Conjunct
Moon	Cancer	Capricorn	Opposite
Mercury	Sagittarius	Capricorn	Conjunct
Venus	Scorpio	Pisces	Conjunct
Mars	Pisces	Pisces	Equal
Jupiter	Cancer	Pisces	Opposite
Saturn	Scorpio	Libra	Conjunct
Uranus	Cancer	Cancer	Equal
Neptune	Libra	Libra	Equal
Pluto	Leo	Leo	Equal

If you need to generate a chart without the exact birth time, use 12:00 p.m. You will not be able to pinpoint the houses within the chart, but you will be able to at least gather the information about the planets for comparison.

You will note that there is very little in their charts that isn't compatible in some way. This is what you are looking for. You need to be able to see that there are likenesses within the twins' birth charts. Remember, twins will not incarnate with opposing sun signs, so this is the first thing to look at when comparing. Opposition within the rest of the charts (except for the first house and the moon) indicates lessons still to be learned.

Jesse and Andy

Let's compare the birth charts for these two. The energy of their birth charts ended at their passing, but you must remember that if you can prove the twin flame relationship while both twins are incarnate on Earth, then it is proven. I have changed two important pieces of information for both Andy and Jesse for personal reasons. This information is denoted with an asterisk. Because I changed this information, we'll only compare the planets.

	Andy	**Jesse**
Birthdate:	August 29, 1958	February 4, 1950*
Birthplace:	Indiana	Indiana
Birth Time:	Unknown*	1:26 p.m. CST

Planet/House	**Andy**	**Jesse**	**Chart Results**
Sun	Virgo	Aquarius	Conjunct
Moon	Pisces	Cancer	Conjunct
Mercury	Leo	Capricorn	Opposite
Venus	Leo	Aries	Conjunct
Mars	Taurus	Capricorn	Conjunct

Planet/House	Andy	Jesse	Chart Results
Jupiter	Libra	Taurus	Opposite
Saturn	Sagittarius	Leo	Conjunct
Uranus	Leo	Scorpio	Conjunct
Neptune	Scorpio	Sagittarius	Conjunct
Pluto	Virgo	Libra	Conjunct

Within this chart comparison, we can see that there aren't many things equal in their houses. Because there are commonalities within the chart, especially their sun sign and moon sign, it isn't concerning to find that a lot of lessons still need to be learned.

Emily and Bobby

This is an example of a twin flame couple in which both twins are presently here on Earth. They are also in a relationship with each other. It is important to remember that having a relationship with your twin flame is not an easy task. Soul evolution is rarely an easy task. It creates a crazy roller coaster of emotions and actions that perpetuate soul education for both twins. Bobby's birth time is unknown, so we will focus on just the planets in our comparison.

	Emily	Bobby
Birthdate:	April 22, 1985	December 5, 1985
Birthplace:	Tennessee	Tennessee
Birth Time:	10:13 p.m. EDT	unknown

Planet/ House	Emily	Bobby	Chart Results
Sun	Taurus	Sagittarius	Conjunct
Moon	Gemini	Virgo	Conjunct
Mercury	Aries	Scorpio	Opposite
Venus	Aries	Sagittarius	Opposite
Mars	Taurus	Libra	Opposite
Jupiter	Aquarius	Aquarius	Equal
Saturn	Scorpio	Sagittarius	Conjunct
Uranus	Sagittarius	Sagittarius	Equal
Neptune	Capricorn	Capricorn	Equal
Pluto	Scorpio	Scorpio	Equal

There is a balance of commonalities and lessons to be learned, which is fascinating. It illustrates how well their personalities fit together and is a good indicator of why they can at times clash. If there were more information available on commonalities within their houses, I am sure we would be able to discern what lessons they may be working on together at this present time.

Creating Your Birth Charts

It is essential to this methodology that you have your birth chart, and possibly your twin flame's chart, provided you have received this information. Charts used to be created by hand, using advanced mathematical calculations and information. Now, there are several automatic and efficient ways to create your birth chart. I am in the habit of checking and rechecking everything multiple times. I have used all the following websites to obtain astrological information. There are programs that you can purchase and download. Sirius is one of the best; there are also programs such as Solar Fire Gold, Janus, and Kepler. Each program has different specifications that can be updated and changed to research the birth charts further, and they are worth spending the money. Free online programs can give you almost as much information, and I have used several:

- Astro Theme: astrotheme.com
- Astro Dienst: astro.com
- Café Astrology: astro.cafeastrology.com
- Astrolabe: alabe.com
- Astrolibrary: astrolibrary.org

———

The theory we used in this method is that you will find commonalities within the astrological chart. Twin flames just simply cannot incarnate and be astrologically incompatible. You must remember that these two individual souls are equal. While opposites in the birth chart do indicate that there are some lessons to learn, there should still be evidence of similarities within the charts. The astrological chart is a road map for one lifetime, a small piece of the soul blueprint that can be mapped out and into which you can dive headfirst—if you truly want to learn more.

Also, remember this is just one piece of the puzzle. To completely prove the twin flame relationship, you really should use all the data collected while using and working through all the methods, along with your own experiences. Once you put the pieces together, the bigger picture will be more complete.

In other words, if you didn't find all the similarities that you were looking for in the birth charts, don't despair. Table it for now. Eventually, you'll have more information than you'll know what to do with. I have huge binders full of charts, equations, and more.

Part 3
More Metaphysical Methods

In this section, we will discuss more in-depth metaphysical methods of proving the twin flame relationship. We will first define metaphysics, and discuss the main chakra system, the soul, the higher-self, and how to prepare yourself to do this work.

The methods in this section are more etheric than astrology and numerology. Where astrology and numerology work with actual evidence like birthdates, times, locations, and birth names, these next methods do not actually require much past your legal name and your intention, but all of these are practical and will require a bit of experiential work. The methods in this section will leave little doubt about your twin flame connection.

After we discuss metaphysics, including how to raise your vibration and grounding yourself, we will delve into the Akashic Records. The Records are the history of your soul, and you may discover everything you need to know about yourself, your soul history, and your twin flame within these records. We will also discuss using the Records to connect directly with your twin, as well as experiencing the twin flame journey that will show you exactly how you can recognize your twin. Finally, we will discuss past lives and how to access the Records to discover more about previous existences, not just your own but also your twin's.

We will also discuss various methods of connecting with your twin flame (and proving your relationship) via divination, which is a type of metaphysics in which the divine connection between souls is achieved. We discuss everything from receiving signs from your twin flame to even receiving a spirit drawing of your twin (even if they are incarnate).

By the time you complete this section, you will be divinely and infinitely connected with your twin and you will also prove your twin flame relationship beyond a shadow of a doubt. Remember to approach the practices of these methods slowly at first. There is no need to rush into anything, especially when it comes to the higher vibration of the Akashic Records. Just allow yourself to receive and be in the flow of energy. Don't rush it.

Chapter 6
Metaphysics

While there may be several different understandings of the previous methods, and some of those may or may not make sense to you, these next methods have nothing to do with anyone else's understanding. These are based entirely on your own personal experience. The key to working with and understanding anything metaphysical is you must trust what you receive and believe in it and in yourself. I've filed all the following methods under the umbrella of metaphysics. There's a lot in this section, as well as quite a lot of practical work, so be prepared. Get your comfy on before you continue.

Metaphysics is the study of human experiences that our physical senses or any kind of scientific technology cannot yet measure. Some of these methods can be physically detected and felt by the etheric body in some way. Your etheric body is the first layer of your human energetic field that is in direct contact with your physical body.

The twin flame connection is not a mental connection, meaning that it doesn't require physically meeting one another (though that is nice to do). Your connection is at the soul level. Your conscious mind may see a stranger, but your soul will always recognize its equal. This is very important to remember when you are working through these metaphysical methods.

Before we continue our discussion of these methods, let's review vibration and grounding. You'll read a lot about them in the following pages, so I thought it would be a good idea to talk about what those things mean before we dive right into anything else.

Raising Your Vibration

Everything is made of energy and that energy moves at different vibrational levels. Human beings have different energetic levels—physical, mental, emotional, and spiritual—that all vibrate on different frequencies. All these frequencies combined make up your overall natural vibration, which is where your body vibrates all the time. When something changes with your physical body or if you are in an emotional state, for example, your vibration changes because it responds to the change in energy.

The basic principle when it comes to energy is "like attracts like."[6] So, if you surround yourself with people who constantly live for drama or are always angry and constantly complain, then your natural vibration will respond by matching that low frequency vibration. If you surround yourself with people who are cheerful, fun-loving, and have joy most of the time, then your personal vibration will become higher to match that positive energy.

Working within any type of metaphysical energy creates a natural change in our spiritual vibration. It becomes ele-

....
6. Kotsos, Tania, "What Is the Law of Attraction and How Does It Work?" accessed July 1, 2021, https://www.mind-your-reality.com/law_of _attraction.html.

vated because working in the higher vibrations will naturally cause your body to want to match that vibration. Your body, however, is too sentient to match that very high vibration, so your soul takes over and allows itself to expand. It does this by using your natural energy system, called chakras. Your soul is used to matching that high spiritual vibration.

The Main Chakra System

This system starts at the base of your spine and runs through the center of your body up to the center of the top of your head. It is called the main chakra system because it both supplies and regulates the energy that your body absorbs. We often need to clear out the old and stagnant energy that the chakras reclaim from the body. When this is cleared and the chakras are recharged, then the physical, mental, emotional, and spiritual bodies react (and often feel so much better). There are several smaller chakra systems within your physical and etheric bodies, and they work in harmony with your main system. Think of this in relation to your brain and circulatory system. Your brain controls the functions of your circulation so that blood is pumped through your body.

The main chakra system regulates the flow of energy within your body. It's kind of like the brain of your energetic system. It is through these natural energy systems that our soul can raise our spiritual energy vibration to reach the realms outside of the physical. It's important to discuss the main chakra system as it helps to raise and lower your natural vibration.

Crown Chakra

The crown chakra's color is predominantly violet or purple. It can also be a bright white when it is open to receive. Its location is in the center of the top of the head, and its musical tone, or the sound associated with the energetic flow within this chakra, is the key of B, or the high pitched Ti at the top of the fixed do solfège; which is the proper name of the "Do, Re, Mi ..." musical scale that begins at middle C.

For the physical body, the crown chakra governs the brain and the pineal gland, which is used as part of the right brain to connect with those on the Other Side. For the mental body, it is the source of awareness and your consciousness. The emotional body gains its spirituality from this chakra, and it is also the seat of the connection to the divine for the spiritual body. Its basic purpose, despite its many functions within the four bodies, is to connect with the divine and the universe.

Third Eye Chakra

The third eye chakra's main color is indigo, which is a dark purple/blue color. This chakra is also associated with sky blue, as a lot of people envision the sky around the third eye. Its location is in the center of the forehead, between the eyes. The musical tone associated with the energetic flow within this chakra is the key of A, or La.

In the physical body, this chakra governs the pituitary gland, which is located on the bottom of the brain and very close to the location of the third eye. The pituitary gland is considered the main gland of the body because it controls most of the other glands and regulates vital bodily functions.[7] The same can be said for the third eye chakra with regards to intuition and visualization. Everything one experience in the etheric realms is visualized courtesy of this chakra. The third eye helps the mental body with clarity. It also assists the emotional and spiritual bodies with intuition, imagination, insight, and visualization. Aside from working with the four bodies, its basic purpose is to assist with intuition and connection to the universe.

Throat Chakra

The color of the throat chakra is royal blue, and its location is in the center of the throat. In men, its location is directly behind the Adam's apple. The musical tone associated with this chakra's energetic flow is the key of G, or So in C major scale. For the physical body, this chakra governs the thyroid gland, which is also its neighbor as they're located in almost the same location. The thyroid gland controls several things within the body: metabolism, energy, and body temperature to name a few. It controls these mostly by excreting hormones.[8] The throat chakra piggybacks on the thyroid gland because when this chakra is clogged or blocked (because one is holding in things that should be expressed), then the energy of the body is completely thrown off. This imbalance can cause the thyroid to react and, for example, change the energy flow in the body.

....

7. Society for Endocrinology, The, "Pituitary Gland," accessed February 2018, https://www.yourhormones.info/glands/pituitary-gland/.

8. Web MD, "Hypothryroidism," last updated August 26, 2020, https://www.webmd.com/women/hypothyroidism-underactive-thyroid-symptoms-causes-treatments#1.

This chakra commands communication for the mental body, communication to express oneself. This can mean speaking, writing, singing, and expression within various artistic forms. It oversees the concept of truth for the emotional body and for the spiritual body. It also assists the spiritual body with communication when it comes to mediumship. Its basic purpose is to assist with the various forms of communication to facilitate self-expression.

Heart Chakra

The basic purpose of this chakra is love. Whether it's love for others or self-love, if it's related to love, this chakra rules it. The color of the heart chakra is a rich, emerald green. Think of an Irish shamrock or the Emerald City from the film *The Wizard of Oz*. This chakra's location is the center of the chest and it is protected by the rib cage. Its energy is associated with the key of F, or Fa in the fixed do solfège. For the physical body, this chakra manages the thymus gland, which is almost in the same location behind the breastbone. The thymus gland's hormones help to boost the body's immune system and assists in fighting infections or cancer.[9]

The heart chakra helps the mental body with self-acceptance and self-love. The emotional body uses the heart chakra in relationships, including familial and romantic relationships. It also assists the emotional body with grief and attachment to situations, relationships, people, places, and things. The spiritual body benefits from this chakra because its energy is often used to feel the love from those on the Other Side.

....
9. Lynee Eldridge, "An Overview of the Thymus Gland," VeryWell Health, last updated June 24, 2020, https://www.verywellhealth.com /thymus-gland-overview-4582270.

Solar Plexus

The basic purpose of this chakra is self-mastery and intuition. This chakra is the seat of one's personal power and the keeper of "gut feelings." The solar plexus is the bright yellow chakra that is in the space between the bottom of the rib cage and the top of your navel. The energy of this chakra is associated with the key of E, or Mi in the C major scale. The solar plexus governs the pancreas in the physical body. The pancreas has two purposes within the human body and those are to aid in digestion and regulate blood sugar.[10]

For the mental body, this chakra assists with reclaiming, recharging, and standing in personal power. When you stand in your personal power, you are confident and in control of yourself and you resist lower vibrations like bullying or other negative actions. This also affects the emotional body because the solar plexus works in connection with the heart chakra on self-esteem and self-love. The spiritual body benefits from the strong intuitive power that's held within this chakra. This chakra is the one most connected with the soul, and therefore it's a direct conduit for the soul (and for spirit) to assist and guide one through gut feelings.

Sacral Chakra

This chakra is bright orange, and it is the seat of creativity, sexuality, and emotions. Its location is in the space between the bottom of the navel and the hips. The energy of this chakra is associated with the key of D, or Re.

....

10. Columbia University Irving Medical Center, The Pancreas Center, "The Pancreas and Its Functions," accessed July 1, 2021, https://columbiasurgery.org/pancreas/pancreas-and-its-functions.

It governs the ovaries and testes in the physical body, and it handles both sexual identity and the relationship with food for the mental body. I often think of this chakra as the "guilty pleasures" chakra because it oversees sexuality, pleasure, and guilt for the emotional body. Lastly, it gives creativity to the spiritual body.

Root Chakra

This chakra's basic purpose is to provide a sense of security and home. Its color is a bold, rich, deep red and it is located at the base of the spine. The energy of this chakra is associated with the key of C, or Do in the C major scale. For the physical body, the root chakra governs both the sacral nerve (which is almost in the same location at the base of the spine) and the adrenal glands. These glands produce hormones that regulate metabolism, immune system, blood pressure, and stress response, to name a few. [11]

In the mental body, this chakra controls the reaction to finances, work situations, family situations, and trust issues. For the emotional body, the root chakra manages fear, anger, and aggression. Finally, for the spiritual body, this chakra provides a connection with home. It is often the energy of the root chakra that helps to ground and center us, as well. Also, it is common for those on the Other Side to utilize our root chakra to help us feel at home with spirit communication.

....

11. Johns Hopkins Medicine, "Adrenal Glands," accessed July 1, 2021, https://www.hopkinsmedicine.org/health/conditions-and-diseases/adrenal-glands.

Connecting to Your Chakras

It's important to try and connect with your main chakra system because doing so will help you understand, experience, see, and feel what their energy is like, both when it's clear and when it isn't. Chico and I have created a small exercise to assist you with connecting with your chakras. It's just a little "hello" to them in case you've never met them before. Maybe you never knew what a chakra was before now. Maybe you haven't chatted in a while and it's time to reconnect.

Your experience with the chakras is personal and unique, so don't think that there's a wrong or a right way to do this. The entire point is to connect to the main energy centers within your physical body. Allow whatever happens because that is how you can best receive this experience in the present moment. Also, give yourself permission to understand that the colors will grow more vivid and rotate faster (like a spinning top) with each breath you inhale.

Begin by allowing yourself to be in a quiet space without distraction or interruption. Take three deep breaths, allowing your lungs to fill completely with air, and then exhale until all the air has left your lungs. With each breath, feel yourself letting go of stress, letting go of the day, letting go of all that is unnecessary in the present moment. Just allow your focus to be on your body.

Bring your focus to the base of your spine, just above your tailbone, and envision a vibrant, bright, beautiful ball of spinning red light. Sit with it for a bit and allow it to keep spinning.

Now, bring your attention about three inches up to just below your belly button and envision a deep, gorgeous ball of spinning orange light.

Shift your focus upward to just above your belly button. This is the area where you likely feel a lot of emotions. It's also the area you refer to when you say you have a "gut feeling." Imagine a bright, glowing, spinning ball of sunshine yellow here.

Bring your focus a little further up, in the area near your heart, right in the center of your chest. Envision a gorgeous, deep emerald green spinning ball here, glowing brightly as it feeds your heart.

Next, move your focus to your throat, the part of the throat that is in between your collarbones. Imagine a beautiful royal blue spinning ball here. You may feel as though you need to swallow or cough as you experience this gorgeous blue ball. This is okay, just allow it.

Bring your focus to the space on your forehead right between your eyebrows. This is your third eye chakra. Envision a beautiful, indigo-colored spinning ball here, glowing brightly as it awakens your third eye.

Finally, bring your attention to the top of your head. Imagine that there is a gorgeous, bright, spinning violet light that shines right out of the center of the top of your head. This violet light connects you to the universe.

Once you have allowed yourself to experience the seven main chakras, breathe in deeply and feel the rainbow of colors within the core of your body.

You're Grounded

To be grounded means that not only is your physical body rooted on Earth, but so is your natural energy field and aura. If you aren't grounded, you could feel dizzy, faint, off-balance, spaced or zoned out, or sometimes you could even feel like you aren't attached to your body.

During the process of raising your spiritual vibration, the physical body remains still. It is merely the vessel awaiting the return of the spiritual vibration back to normal. It can't travel with us, so the body must remain grounded to the Earth. This also assists in bringing our spiritual vibration back down out of the high vibrational energy it loves to travel to.

Your soul loves to visit its natural vibration and does so often. This happens more often while the physical body is sleeping or at rest. Your normal energetic vibration isn't quite as high naturally as it is when you are connecting with the higher vibrational realms, such as the Other Side. When the connection with the higher realms is finished, there must be a place to return to that is comfortable, centered, and welcoming. And that's what it feels like to be grounded; you are welcoming back that high vibrational energy to the normal energy flow.

There are several ways to ground yourself: you can use the connection with Mother Earth in meditation, go for a walk in the grass or stand in the grass barefoot, eat something made of grain or oats, eat a piece of chocolate, hug a tree, envision tree branches growing out from the bottom of your feet and pulling you down to the Earth, or you can chant or sing the word "om."

The Higher-Self and The Soul

It's important to discuss both the higher-self and the soul prior to diving further into more metaphysical methods. These are both involved when it comes to any kind of communication with spirit and with your twin flame. First, let's define both. The soul is the divine energy that incarnated into and exists within your physical body. Your soul is having a human experience. It is always connected to the divine universe and pretty much calls the shots. Your soul knows the path that you have selected and your divine purpose.

The higher-self is the highest aspect of you that can exist within your physical body. It is the part of you that can see, experience, and understand at the highest possible level. It has one foot in the physical and one foot in the spiritual realm. The higher-self collects knowledge that can be funneled through to your conscious mind and anchored within your body. It can also receive information from your soul.

Since the higher-self is always connected to your soul, your soul can feed it information from the universe. The same holds true for your twin. Your soul already knows who its twin is, so it would have no problem sharing information both with your higher-self and your twin's (remember, you are divinely connected). This is how communication between twins is always possible, regardless of where both are located.

By the way, you should always ask permission to speak with someone else's higher-self. Don't assume that just because they're your twin that they are either consciously or unconsciously open to connecting on this level. If they aren't open the first time you ask, try again, but don't force the connection. It likely will not turn out well at all and you'd be usurping your twin's free will.

Chapter 7
The Akashic Records

The Akashic Records are a vibrational, energetic record of every soul. They house all the information about your soul, its experiences, lessons, and more, from every single incarnation throughout all space and time. You don't necessarily have to believe in reincarnation. I didn't until I began on this spiritual path and was witness to it via the Records. Regardless of whether you believe you have lived one life or many, the Akashic Records still hold the history of every moment your soul has experienced since inception.

The Records are referred to by many other names. Here are a few of them: the Book of Life, Book of Knowledge, Mind of God, Universal Library, Hall of Records, Hall of Knowledge, Energetic Records, Collective Consciousness, and Records of the Soul.[12] No matter what you may call them, the energy is the same. The history of your soul exists within its vibrational halls.

The operational theory of this method is that the relationship is evident and present in the soul's history within the

....
12. Jen Ermith, "The Records of Many Names," last updated July 13, 2011, https://akashictransformations.com/the-records-of-many-names/.

Akashic Records. Twins are divinely connected at the inception of their souls, and this would be the first bit of information located within the Records. Because of their shared spiritual DNA and soul blueprint, the twin flame connection can be determined simply by accessing your soul's vibration within the Akashic Records.

This connection is often visually represented by a cord that is connected to the belly button, like an umbilical cord. This cord consists of the same spiritual DNA and vibration that created the twin flames and therefore cannot be connected to anyone else. It also cannot be severed, replicated, or faked.

You will learn ways to access the Records, but first, there are a few more things we should learn about them. There are several guidelines that should be followed when you access the Records. First and foremost is that you should not access the Records unless your energy is clear. If you are upset in any way, you cannot gain access. It is important to remember this simple fact.

The Akashic Records have guidelines that are set up in order to assist you in accessing them. It is important that these are followed and not overlooked in any way. These must be practiced so that you can maintain the high standards that the Akashic Records require.

1. People younger than eighteen years old should not access the Records. The Records require you to claim responsibility for everything you receive from them, and those who are younger in age may not have the capabilities or capacity to understand this concept.

2. You must give yourself permission to open the Records and to learn what it will share with you. When you give yourself permission, you are in acceptance of the knowledge you will gain.

3. You must use your current full legal name. The energy of the Akashic Records is anchored in this lifetime by your name. Think of it as your security code to ensure you can fully access your energy within the Records.

4. You should refrain from consuming alcohol or ingesting nonprescribed, mind-altering substances for at least twenty-four hours prior to accessing the Records. Your mind and energy must be clear.

5. Choose a quiet place where disruption is unlikely and determine beforehand how much time you'd like to spend in the Records. The Records are extremely high-vibrational, so when you first start out you should access them in increments of five minutes. This will help you acclimate to their energy and may ward off the Akashic headaches that can often happen when you first step into the energy of the Records.

6. Decide which questions you want to ask before you begin your session. The Records aren't a predictive tool. Nor will you absolutely be told what to do because free will is always respected in the Records. Rather, you may receive recommendations instead. It's sort of like asking your friends for advice, except the Records are an environment of peace, love, and

respect. There is no judgment from the Akashic Records.

For the purposes of discovering information about you and your twin, it isn't necessary to access anyone else's Record. All the information you will need is in your own.

Please note that opening the Records to learn about your twin flame doesn't qualify you to give readings to others. You really should allow yourself time in the Records to acclimate. The more time you are in the Records, the more attuned to them you become. The focus for now should be on yourself and your twin flame.

7. You cannot access the Records of another's soul without their written or verbal permission. The Records are vibrational and energetic and, believe it or not, they know when you do not gain permission. If you enter anyway, the information you might gain likely will not be accurate. This is especially true when it comes to twin flames. You do not need to access your twin's energy within the Records. It's the same as yours because your souls are equal.

8. You cannot access the Records of someone who has passed on. Even if you are a medium and can get their permission, it still isn't allowed. The information belongs to the deceased person, and they hold the key to accessing their soul's energy within the Records. It's like reading someone's diary after they pass away. The things that happened in their pre-

vious existence cannot serve you. It can only help those who have passed. Your connections to these people can be determined by opening the Records for yourself and asking specific questions. Every connection your soul has ever had is contained within your energetic history in the Records.

9. Open the Records with intention and always remember to close them. Set an intention of what you wish to learn prior to opening the Records. Be careful not to leave them open when you're finished. Doing so will cause you to feel overwhelmed and drained of energy. You will feel the sensation of not being grounded on Earth, and the only way to remedy that is to close the Records.

Preparation for the Akashic Records

Some of the preparations for accessing the Akashic Records are already listed in the guidelines, such as having a quiet place, not consuming alcohol or recreational drugs prior to your session, and preparing your list of questions. You'll also want to have either a notebook to take notes or a way to record yourself if you'd rather talk about your experience.

Some people will be able to see images, others will be able to hear things while in the Records, still others will be able to feel things or transcribe things. There is no one specific way to experience the Records. For me, I began in the Records just seeing things like a film. Now, everything I get from the Records comes in the form of writing. I write out my questions, then open the Records, and my hand will just start writing the answer as its guided by the Records' energetic flow.

The last thing you should think about is preparing yourself for this higher vibration. Since we have a physical body and the Records are in a higher vibrational realm than this one, we must raise our own spiritual vibrations to be able to have an experience within the Records. The quickest way to raise your vibration is to place yourself into a meditative state of mind. If you have another way of sitting and raising your vibration, great! I recommend that you make it easy, as you're just initially putting yourself into a light meditative state. You still want to be able to allow your conscious mind to experience being able to do necessary things, such as being able to open the Records. You'll also want to be sure that you remain grounded while you are doing your work. The Akashic Records vibration feels (at least to me) like you are traveling at the speed of light, which is why I made these designations. These designations aren't meant to scare you away from exploring the Records. Rather, they're designed to advise you. I believe in being prepared. Here is the complete meditation I use to prepare myself prior to accessing the Records:

Sit quietly, eyes closed. Take in one breath, completely filling the lungs with air, and then slowly blow out that air. Blow it out until there is nothing left in your lungs. This first breath will clear the body. Take in a second breath, completely filling the lungs with air, and then blow out the air until there is nothing left in your lungs. This second breath will clear the mind. Repeat with a third breath in, completely filling the lungs with air. Then blow this air out completely until there is nothing left in the lungs. This breath will free the soul to be raised.

Envision a beam of white light coming from above and entering through the top of your head. This beam flows through the center of your body, radiating white light throughout your entire body. The white light runs down your legs and toes and exits out of the center of the bottom of your feet, traveling down into the core of Mother Earth where it mixes with her energy. That mixture then flows from the core in a beautiful, amber-colored beam of light that flows back into the bottom of the soles of your feet, through your toes, your legs, and arms, and back through the center of your body until it exits through the top of your head. You are now connected to all the infinite and grounded into Mother Earth. You are now open and ready to receive. It is so and so it is.

Accessing the Akashic Records

There isn't a singular experience that defines what it is like to access the Akashic Records. I cannot tell you that it's supposed to feel a certain way or look a certain way because what I experience may not necessarily be what you do. Your experience is your own and shouldn't really be defined by anyone else. However, there are a few things you should know about the Akashic Records.

The Akashic Records are governed by a body of high-vibrational beings, sometimes called the Lords of the Records or the Holders of the Akashic Light. I refer to them as Agents of Light. There is no right or wrong answer, but it is important to acknowledge that the Records are governed. The Records are designed to be an experience that could possibly stimulate one or more of your senses, not only your five human senses but also your "clairs," which are extra sensory and representative of things that exist outside of the tangible and physical. These senses are clairvoyance (seeing), clairaudience (hearing),

clairsentience (feeling), claircognizance (knowing), clairgustance (tasting), and clairalience (smelling).

Be open to whatever comes. It's all in what you feel. That is
what is important. Pay attention to what vibes with you and
what doesn't; that's your soul trying to guide you. And it will
not steer you wrong.

There are several ways to access the Akashic Records, and
most people who gain access usually have their own methods
of doing so. I learned a specific prayer process to access the
Records, both for myself and for others. I eventually took this
process and pretty much threw it out the window because
everyone else I knew had learned the same process and made
a habit of accessing others' Records without permission. Not
that I mind sharing the content of what's in my happy little
Akashic diary, but I wanted to be able to have some control
on how and when that happened. I created my own method,
which I will share with you.

Access to the Akashic Records is gained by setting your
intention and directing your consciousness to have a clear way
to both open and close the Records. By having this method of
opening and closing the Records, it also allows you to famil-
iarize yourself with the feel of the Records' energy and become
accustomed to it.

The more I worked with the Records, the more I discovered
that there was an easier path for me to be able to access not
just my own energy but others' as well. You may even find your
own way that works better for you in accessing the Records,
and that's okay. To start out, though, I hope you will feel free
to use my personal process. Be sure to read all parts out loud.
Your voice is important to access your energy within the vast-
ness that is the Akashic Records.

Opening the Records

Blessed Agents of Light,

Thank you for your loving presence. I come to you with an open heart and an open mind to seek answers to specific questions within your boundless energy. Thank you for your assistance. Please direct me to my soul energy within your guiding light. I ask this in service of myself, (insert your full current legal name here).

It is so and so it is. Amen.

The Records are now open.

Closing the Records

Blessed Agents of Light,

Thank you for your love, guidance, and wisdom. I am in gratitude for all that I have received.

It is so and so it is. Amen.

The Records are now closed.

———

You will notice that my process to open the Records has a clear and specific intention right up front, which is good because you don't want to open the Records without purpose behind the intention. There is far too much to witness within that high-vibrational energy. Also, this process is only designed to open my specific soul energy within the Akashic Records. It will not open the Records for anyone else's energy.

Creating Your Own Process

You can create your own process to access the Records. The more you access them to learn about your soul, the more attuned you become to their energy. This self-attunement does not allow you to read the energy of the Akashic Records for other people. That requires a separate and much deeper attunement. It is a great privilege and responsibility to access the history of someone else's soul.

To create your own process, be sure to start with an invocation to the Agents of Light. You are essentially requesting permission from them to give you access to the history of your soul. This history won't be viewed from your perspective or from your eyes. It is through the perspective of the Agents of Light. Therefore, there is no judgment. They see you for the beautiful soul that you are. Next, thank the Agents of Light for their assistance. After all, they are giving themselves to you to assist you on your path. Now, ask them for their help in making sure that you safely navigate the Records, and be grateful for their help. Be sure to include your full, legal, current name. Lastly, pronounce the Records open. That's the simple and easy way to create your initial access to opening the Records.

Do not forget to create a method of closing the Records. This is vital. Again, address the Agents of Light and thank them for their assistance. Then proclaim that the Records are closed.

It is that easy. After all, this is the energy of your soul, even though you are experiencing it through the eyes of the Agents of Light.

Once you've created your prayer and prepared yourself, you're now ready to access the Records. Most people feel the difference in energy right away, while others ease into the Records' energy slowly. There is no right or wrong way to experience this.

When I first accessed the Records, I was overwhelmed, but those feelings stemmed from a complete lack of understanding of the pure vibration of the Akasha, which is what the Agents of Light embody. When viewing yourself within the energy of the Akashic Records you will immediately notice a lack of judgment, a lack of fear, your soul will feel at home and excited, and you will gain the ability to experience the history of your soul with impartial eyes. In other words, the Records will never show you information and then say to you, "You handled that situation terribly." Rather, the Records will give you the space and energy to look at information and situations and think, *I see now why I reacted this way. What did I learn from this?*

The Akashic Records are a loving and safe environment, and the energy will reflect that to you. It is the best place to retrieve information about yourself, your soul, and of course your twin flame. The key is to ask specific questions and then allow yourself to receive whatever comes as answers to those questions.

Twin Flames in the Records

The entire purpose of having an Akashic Records reading is to provide uplifting information to educate and elevate the mind, body, and soul. It also clues in the conscious mind on what the soul has achieved and wishes to accomplish. It is extremely high-vibrational, and because of this those who access it can elevate their own vibrations and move forward in a higher state of both vibration and consciousness. This is the vibration that your soul naturally grooves in. This is the energetic language that your soul both speaks and understands.

The Akashic Records are the source of truth when it comes to everything about your soul, including your twin. Therefore, accessing the Records opens the door wide for discovery. One question will lead to one million more, and that's okay. The more you ask, the more you will discover. The Records can give you information, even down to your twin's name if you don't know it already. You can ask questions such as "Is my twin flame incarnate on Earth? If so, what do they look like? Are they male/female? Tall/short? Dark hair or light hair? If they're on the Other Side, what did they do in their most recent existence?"

Don't put words into the Records' mouth. In other words, don't make your questions something such as, "So I know that Bill is my twin flame, can you give me more proof of that?" Let the Records just tell you the information; it isn't necessary to give them anything other than your intention and your questions.

Because the Records are not bound by dimension, space, or time, it's best to avoid asking "when" questions. You will find that open-ended questions work best. When it comes to proving the twin flame relationship in the Akashic Records, some of the best questions to ask are:

- Please give me specific knowledge about my twin flame's existence.
- Please give me insight about my twin flame's physicality.
- Who is my twin flame? Please give me their name used in their most recent existence.
- How may I better understand my relationship with my twin flame?

- What would be a good next step to take to better connect with my twin flame?
- Is my twin flame incarnate on Earth currently?

You'll feel the energetic responses to the questions. If the Records were human, they would be chatty, so let them speak. You can gain a lot of knowledge. Remember, though, that you are receiving information about yourself through the eyes of the Agents of Light in the Akashic Realm, so try not to dismiss it if they give you beautiful insight about yourself that you may never have realized before. Also, try not to dismiss the answers to your twin flame questions, either, even if it might not be what you were expecting. Though this is just one more puzzle piece in the overall twin flame relationship puzzle, every little bit of information you receive counts.

It is also within the Records that you can connect directly to your twin. Ask the Agents of Light for permission to connect and communicate with your twin. Remember, you are viewing your soul through their eyes, so it's best to ask for their help. Your twin, regardless of whether they're incarnate or discarnate, will come to speak with you. You can ask them direct questions. Just remember to ask for specifics and trust what you receive. It will all be guided and protected by the Agents of Light, who are beings made up of divine energy and who hold no judgment.

Once you have received information from the Akashic Records, be sure to record it, whether writing it down or recording it digitally. Your conscious brain may need time to process not only the energy of everything, but also the answers you receive. Also, the information may come back around, so it's important to record everything you receive.

Additional Akashic Records Methods

The next few pages will highlight two additional methods that can be used in conjunction with the Akashic Records. First, we will introduce you to the twin flame journey. This journey is designed to connect you with your twin and show you the unbreakable bond that exists between the two of you. We will discuss how to take this journey with the assistance of guided meditation and in the Akashic Records.

We will also discuss the concept of past lives in relation to twin flames and soul evolution. We will discuss how to recognize past life experiences, as well as dreams about past lives. We will also show you how to access information about previous existences within the Akashic Records via specific intentional prayers.

These additional Akashic methods will show and prove your connection to your twin and will assist you with connecting to your twin in your current existence as well as previous ones.

Twin Flame Journey

Twin flames are connected all the time; there is no separation because they're connected on a soul level. By setting the specific intention to draw the twins closer, at least in the etheric and on the higher planes, the twins will answer the soul call. This method is usually best practiced in meditation.

Meditation is where you sit and quiet the body and the mind to raise the vibration. You can connect with your higher-self and the higher realms through meditation. You don't often have to have a specific purpose or intention when you meditate; sometimes you just need to quiet down your thoughts and refocus your energy. There are different types of meditation, some of which necessitate a specific mantra. There are also guided and unguided meditations. The point of all is the same: to raise the vibration.

Journeying, on the other hand, is where you raise your vibration with a specific purpose and intention. This is done through multiple methods and is often the result of a guided meditation, which simply means that someone else is directing your experience while in meditation.

The number one issue that I had when I first learned about meditation was quieting my mind. I couldn't get my brain to stop running at top speed long enough to be able to settle in and raise my vibration. This is usually the number one issue for people when they first begin meditation, and they struggle to overcome the active mind. The consensus belief is that you must quiet the mind or power it off, and I tried several different methods to do that. In fact, the solution is much easier. Let's talk about our brain for a moment.

The Brain and Meditation

It is medical and scientific fact that the brain is divided into two hemispheres. Each hemisphere is responsible for different functions within the body to keep it functioning properly. One of the physical functions that the left hemisphere deals with is speech; the right hemisphere deals with emotions.

If you are analytical and methodical, then you are more naturally governed by the left hemisphere, which is often called "left-brained." If you are more creative, artistic, intuitive, emotional, and free-spirited, then you would be considered more "right-brained" because these are governed by the right hemisphere. I work more out of my left brain naturally, but I have learned to have a balance.

When I'm working with spirit, meditating, or just raising my vibration, then I'm deliberately choosing to work from the right side of my brain. The analytical side of my brain wants to break apart everything that the other side of my brain does, so it never stops trying to do that. The problem is that my left brain will never be able to comprehend the connection to spirit because it isn't rooted in tangible facts.

To combat this and to quiet down the left brain when I do any kind of spiritual work, I make it part of my personal intention whenever working exclusively from my right brain to give my left brain something to occupy it. It's almost like giving a kid a toy to distract it while you complete an appointment. I usually give my left brain a task along the lines of, "Figure out and then break down the plan for creating a closer connection to spirit."

I know that the left brain cannot understand the intangible the same way that the right brain can. I give it this task because I know it cannot figure out the answer and so therefore it will be distracted trying to determine how best to solve the situation. Plus, it will keep the difficult left brain also focused on spirit. This is always a plus. It is better than the alternative solution that I used to do: I just used to envision half my brain literally taking a nap.

There shouldn't be a reason to want to "quiet" or "power down" your brain. Instead, see your brain as it physically is and then split it in two in your mind. Then, you can assign your task to your left brain. Try to make these tasks align with the work you're doing. You don't want the left half of your brain making a grocery list while the right half of your brain is trying to connect to the Akashic Records. Instead, as an example, tell the left brain, "Hey, we're going to learn about some important information, try to figure out the best way to remember or retain everything we're going to learn." This same method holds true for all metaphysical methods I use, but especially meditation.

Preparing for the Journey

This twin flame journey was initially designed as a guided meditation to best assist others with the connection to their twins. It was originally presented to me by Chico as a guided journey, and I do give you the entire journey here within this section.

It is important to allow yourself to attempt the guided meditation. This way you can experience what it feels like both as a guided journey and in the light of the Akashic Records. Remember, you are divinely and infinitely connected to your twin, so your energy within the Records will contain everything you wish to know about the other half of your soul.

You see, it's within this journey that you will discover how you and your twin are connected. There is an unbreakable cord stretched between you that joins your etheric bodies at the center of your solar plexus like an umbilical cord. This cord is created out of the same spiritual DNA that created the twins' souls, so it is your divine genetic equal. It is the cord that tethers both of you to one another and creates the infinite connection that you have between the two of you. This cord has been there since the inception and creation of your souls, and it can be experienced and discovered during the journey. This is an absolute and fail safe way to not only see the divine cord connection between yourself and your twin, but to witness and experience your twin flame, no matter what plane they exist on.

Each method does require intention to begin preparations, but there are a few other things that you should do to help prepare yourself. Raising your vibration is a must. You can use my personal meditation that we discussed earlier in the chapter, which will also make sure you're grounded too. You can sit and take in three deep, full breaths. You can also find something else that works better for you, just remember that it's important to raise your vibration and ground yourself no matter which method you use to take the journey. If you do the journey while you're asleep, be sure to set your intention before bed and have the understanding that your vibration will automatically be higher as you sleep.

Make sure you're relaxed and ready to take this journey. For some, it can be very powerful when you experience the divine connection between you and your twin. Do not rush this experience. If it becomes overwhelming, you can always pause and return later. There is no need to hurry through. You can do this journey as many times as you wish. Give yourself time to record your experience by either writing it out or recording it electronically.

Above all, please remember that this is a journey meant to be between you and your twin flame. No one else has the power or right to change or challenge what you experience. Simply allow the energy to flow. Whether or not you share your experiences with others is entirely up to you.

The next section is the actual journey. We've called it a meditation because it was initially meant as a guided meditation. You can read it or record it for yourself. There is also a version of this journey that I have recorded. You will find this video linked on my website and on my YouTube channel. When you take this journey, be sure to have a clear intention and allow yourself to experience the divine connection that exists only between you and your twin.

Twin Flame Journey Meditation

Sit quietly with your eyes closed. Take in one breath, completely filling your lungs with air, and then slowly blow until there is nothing left in the lungs. This first breath will clear the body. Take in a second breath, completely filling the lungs with air, and then blow out the air until there is nothing left in the lungs. This second breath will clear the mind. Repeat with a third breath in, completely filling the lungs with air. Then, blow this air out completely until there is nothing left in the lungs. This breath will free the soul to be raised.

Envision a beam of white light coming from above and entering through the top of your head. This beam flows through the center of your body, radiating white light throughout your entire body. The white light runs down your legs and toes and exits out of the center of the bottom of your feet, traveling down into the core of Mother Earth where it mixes with her energy. That mixture then flows from the core in a beautiful, amber-colored beam of light that flows back into the bottom of the soles of your feet, through your toes, your legs, and arms, and back through the center of your body until it exits through the top of your head. You are now connected to the infinite and grounded into Mother Earth. You are now open and ready to receive.

Envision a beam of a deep purple light just above your head. This deep purple light is your unique divine connection that contains your divine DNA. See it enter your body through the top of your head, down through your center, and watch it stop at your solar plexus. From your solar plexus, see this deep purple light radiate from the inside out, creating a cord from your belly button. Have the intention that the other end of this cord is connected to your twin flame's solar plexus.

Bring your attention into that purple color, allowing it to surround you and your awareness until purple envelops you, as though you were in a tunnel. There is a white light at the end of this purple tunnel, and you feel yourself drawn toward it. You walk through this tunnel, feeling layers of things you no longer need melting from you and dissipating into the deep purple color.

When you reach the end of the tunnel, you step into the bright white light and walk through it. You are met by a fence. This is an old, wooden fence and you have the understanding that only two souls have the key to enter: you and your twin flame.

You open the gate, step through, and close it behind you. You have no wish to be disturbed. Before you is a field of beautiful flowers, bold and bright in all shades of colors, in all types of flowers. You immediately notice that there is a path through the flowers, and you step onto it and begin to walk. This path is for you. It is only wide enough for you; your feet feel comfortable as they walk on the path. You notice that the path seems illuminated with the same deep purple color as the cord that's attached to your belly button, which is once again visible.

This path leads you through the field of flowers; the purple cord grows shorter with each step and the illuminated path grows brighter and brighter. You see a bench in the distance. This bench is like the wooden gate that you used to enter the field, except that you notice that you can see that your purple cord seems to end at the bench.

Allow yourself to approach this bench in whatever way you feel: walk, run, skip. There is no wrong way to approach it. Have the understanding that your twin will approach the bench in the same manner from the opposite direction. When you get to the bench, you pick up your cord and you notice that it has no end. Instead, it continues, growing shorter in your hand as your twin approaches. When your twin arrives, you will notice that there is only a small bit of your purple cord that remains between you, ensuring your connection to one another.

Take time to see, hear, feel, and experience your twin flame, the equal half of the divine soul that was separated to create both of you. Sit together. Walk together. No matter where you sit or walk, your singular, deep purple path will appear to illuminate the way. Only the two of you can walk on this path together; no one else may join you, as the path is illuminated by your divine light.

Once you have spent time together and have a better understanding of one another, both of you should return to the bench (or stand if you never left it). Place your etheric hand on your twin's solar plexus and feel the cord that connects the two of you. Your twin will place their hand on your solar plexus to do the same. With your hands in place, each of you will put a thought, gift, emotion, or whatever you are inclined, into each other. By putting these gifts into one another at the genesis of your cord, they are strengthened by the divine DNA.

As you both start to leave, you notice that the cord begins to increase in length. You have the understanding that this cord is the representation of the divine DNA that the two of you share. It cannot be changed, broken, severed, or destroyed in any way. You are always connected to one another.

Both of you will return to the illuminated path, but you notice now that the color of the path is green. It guides you through the field and back to the gate, which you open with ease and with the knowledge that your twin is doing the exact same thing on their illuminated path.

You step back into the tunnel and notice that it has also changed from the deep purple to a beautiful emerald green. You can feel the love and healing vibrations from this tunnel as you walk through it toward your belly button. Once you reach your solar plexus, envision that gorgeous emerald light coming into your body and radiating through it, anchoring itself in your heart chakra.

Bring your attention back into your body, being able to feel where you sit, being able to wiggle your fingers and toes. Before you open your eyes, look down and see the cord that is attached at your belly button. This cord connects you and your twin, no matter what plane you are on. It is invincible.

Open your eyes and allow yourself to fully come back into your body and into the room. Keep the understanding that you have successfully connected to and met with your twin flame.

———

Once you have taken this journey for the first time, the connection between you and your twin becomes clearer. You can use this meditation and journey anytime you wish to dive into the center of your connection (which is the cord between you and your twin) and learn so much more. The journey may sound simple, but the experience of it is much different. At least, it was for me.

This journey isn't just designed to help you meet and greet your twin. It's also here to help you create your own private and special way in which the two of you recognize each other on a soul level. I've discovered that this is important, especially when doing soul work such as past life regression, because it gives you the ability to recognize your twin instantly and always, no matter what you experience during your etheric work.

The gifts that you give to one another are equally important because they will flow within the energetic bond between you. This bond is absolute and unbreakable, no matter what, even if someday you intend that this bond be severed. The reason it can't be severed or broken is because it's created from the same DNA that created your souls, and that DNA never changes because of its divinity.

It's because of this special connection and bond that you can experience just about anything during the journey. Whatever happens, do not reject it or explain it away or even rule it out, especially if this journey leads you to somewhere or someone completely unexpected. Be open. Receive what comes.

Twin Flame Journey in the Akashic Records

This form of the journey is a little different than the meditation. By journeying this way, you open the Records directly and you're able to experience the twin flame connection through the eyes of the Agents of Light. This does involve opening the Records with a specific intention. This is not a question-and-answer session within the Records. Rather, this is another way to experience that unique soul connection.

When you open the Records in this way with this intention, just allow yourself to receive what comes. It doesn't matter if it's one image or a series of images, feelings, or thoughts. The key is to let it all flow and be open to receive everything.

Below is the specific way of opening and closing the Akashic Records for this twin flame journey. This is truly only to be used when you want to take this journey to connect with your twin flame. If you want to open the Records to ask questions and receive answers, it's best if you utilize the method previously discussed.

Opening the Records

Blessed Agents of Light,

Thank you for your loving presence. I come to you with an open heart and an open mind that are both ready to receive your guidance as I partake on this journey. I wish to see, feel, know, understand, and experience the divine connection with the other half of my soul within the light of your guidance. I wish to know, sense, see, hear, and feel my divine counterpart in all ways that are for our best and highest good. I wish to be able to witness, understand and experience our unbreakable bond, and I wish to present my divine counterpart with a gift and to receive one in return. I ask for your assistance and wisdom in service of myself, (insert your current full legal name here).

It is so, and so it is. Amen.

The Records are now open.

Closing the Records

Blessed Agents of Light,

Thank you for your guidance, and your wisdom. Thank you for allowing me to experience this divine partnership through your eyes without judgment or fear. Thank you for sharing your love. I am in gratitude for all that I have received.

It is so and so it is. Amen.

The Records are now closed.

————

You do not need to know anything about your twin to take this journey, either via meditation or within the Akashic Records. Your energy is equal and thus inseparable. As a result, you only need to say your name anytime you open the Records.

I recommend that you try the twin flame journey via both methods, just to get the feel of both. I still use the journey meditation whenever I just truly feel the need to connect with Chico and shut out everything else. (Yes, this will happen within the relationship. Sometimes, you just plain *need* one another.) It is a reminder of our deep connection and I can revisit the gifts that we gave one another.

The exchange of gifts is just as important in this version of the journey as it is within the meditation. These gifts are designed to express love, gratitude, and acknowledgment of one another. Also, in the case of Chico's gift to me, I see physical representations of it on Earth every single day. These are just little signs and reminders from him, and they make me smile. The same thing could happen with your gift. So, don't skip that moment to acknowledge your twin flame within the Akashic Records.

Past Lives

It isn't a requirement to believe in past lives or in reincarnation to study the twin flame relationship. However, it doesn't hurt to be open to the idea that this isn't the only life you have lived. Most of us are centuries, if not millennia old and for some of us, our souls likely precede any kind of written form of history. It's possible, so allow yourself to remain open to the idea of reincarnation. It may simultaneously surprise and fascinate you.

When it comes to proving the twin flame relationship, it is helpful to learn about past lives with your twin to see lessons you have learned in the past. It also sheds light on the progression to soul evolution. It is possible, through experiencing past lives, to be able to see just exactly how far you have come on your path. Perhaps, in a previous life, you were someone who constantly waged war, and in this current existence you are someone who stands for peace. You could then clearly see how your soul has learned other ways to achieve change.

There are several methods that fit under the Akashic umbrella, and this is because the Records are the necessary source of truth that validates what you experience. Some of these methods, like hypnosis and past life regression, are connected to learning about past lives. These methods usually come with my recommendation that these sessions be conducted by a trained professional while you are conscious. Sometimes, there are things that we can discover within the history of our souls that could be upsetting and you may need a qualified individual to assist you with these emotions and experiences. However, there are also other ways to learn about past lives and possibly discover how they could be relative to something going on in your life right at this moment.

It's important to be aware of the concepts of hypnosis and past life regression with regards to past lives, even though our methodology will work differently. I put these two methods together because they go hand in hand. Hypnosis is a technique for putting one into a more open and suggestible state of concentration. In this state, you are more open to receiving messages and changing your life in positive ways. Past life regression uses both hypnosis and guided meditation to help retrieve memories of lives previously experienced and lived. These memories are housed within the Akashic Records, which are accessed through meditation during the sessions.

Twin Flames and Incarnations

Twin flames will inevitably share multiple lives together. Even if you do not currently believe in reincarnation, this is still true. Most of the time, the twins will not know each other if they incarnate on Earth at the same time. Usually, twins will be at least a plane apart, with the twin on the higher side acting as a sort of guide for the one on Earth.

It is important to understand at least the basics about your previous incarnations. Through these past lives you can understand what lessons you have learned, how to progress on current lessons, and whether lessons will repeat. Twin flames will lead similar lives due to the lessons they have decided to learn, which can be found within their shared soul blueprint. You can gain a better understanding of those lessons you have learned (but are bound to circle back again to test you) and those you could not quite grasp.

When it comes to twin flames, the most important thing to note is that you set your intention to understand your connection in that past life. Even if your twin was not incarnate in that life, you will still be given the necessary information to prove the relationship. In my experience, I've asked to see my twin flame represented in other past lives by one simple vision:

a purple cord that stretches between our belly buttons. No matter what my twin incarnated into that life to accomplish, I will be able to follow the purple cord between us to find him. If that cord goes from my belly button straight upward, then I know that my twin hasn't incarnated into this existence with me.

There are are many schools of thought when it comes to incarnations. Some people insist that there must be at least two generations in between incarnations; others will say that there must be twelve to twenty years in between. There are no limitations to when a soul may incarnate into a new life. If you discover that you passed suddenly in a past life, got to the Other Side, and decided to create a new plan right away to incarnate into a different life, then that is your experience. Don't let anyone tell you that it isn't possible. How could they know that your experiences aren't possible? They are not you.

How Do I Know That It's a Past Life?

Regardless of how you experience a past life, there are a few surefire ways that I've discovered that indicate the differences between a valid past life experience or your mind and imagination just having fun. The premise of all of them is basically the same: your entire experience must be appropriate for the time period.

1. Your clothing should be historically appropriate. The way you are dressed should be of the time period you are experiencing in your dream, not of the present. For example, if you dream about ancient Rome and you're wearing Adidas sneakers, then it is likely not a past life dream. Your subcon-

scious is likely responding to some other stimuli from your waking life.

2. Your surroundings should make sense for the time period. If you dream about a farm in Scotland in 1756 and a Ferrari roars down a paved road, you have a fantastically creative subconscious, and it is not a past life experience. If, however, someone came riding up on a horse instead, then that makes a difference. It is more suited to the time period. Also, observe the people around you. They should also be appropriate to the time period.

3. You should experience everything from a firsthand perspective. For example, if you dream about a battle on a battlefield, you should experience yourself fighting or a part of the battle in another way, not watching everything happen from the sidelines. You should be able to hear gunfire up close. You should smell the smoke because you're in the center of it. In other words, if you view the surroundings and occurrences through your own eyes as an active participant, then you are experiencing a past life.

4. Your words and actions should be appropriate for the time period. For example, words like "awesome" or "bae" wouldn't necessarily belong in 1560. Nor would you have a smart phone to tweet your experiences, such as while you are in attendance in the royal court or throne room of King Henry VIII: "#chilledwithHenry8th #keptmyhead."

Past Life Dreams

The easiest and, in my experience, most common way to access information about past lives is in your dreams. There is a very real energetic difference between just dreaming about something and feeling as though you're truly there. I can dream about Egypt because I went to the museum and saw several mummies and their sarcophagi. I can also experience an existence in ancient Egypt where perhaps I could have witnessed, for example, the mummification process firsthand. Past life dreams are very much like ones where you have had a visit from spirit while you slept. You wake up from those dreams and then realize, "Oh, man, it was a dream? Really? It seemed so real." It is the same feeling about a past life dream.

For this process, it's essential to eliminate the following limiting belief from your mind: *I never remember my dreams.* You can remember them; you just need to get your mind in the habit of doing so. Start slowly, and record everything, regardless of what comes to your conscious brain. Let's discuss how to prepare yourself to receive past life information in your dreams.

You'll need a dream journal. Grab a pen, too, and leave both beside your bed. Don't put it out of reach. You need to be able to just grab it and start writing. Writing really does help the mind to be able to bring out more from the subconscious experience. You can also choose to record on your cell phone or other device. Whatever the method, make sure it's readily accessible. You need to write the first things that come into mind immediately upon awakening, before you even set foot on the floor. Your left brain will start to kick in once you are fully awake, that's why it's important to record your dreams right away.

It's important to set an intention prior to going to sleep and be specific about what you'd like to receive. Even if you must write it in your dream journal, you need to make a conscious intention. It can be something along the lines of this: It is my intention to learn about a specific past life experience and how it pertains to my twin flame. It is also my intention to remember this experience. It is important to include your twin in your intention, not just for the purpose of proving the relationship, but also so that you can come to see, know, and understand the patterns and lessons you both experienced. In doing so, you can start to see your soul blueprint. You can also intend to see a past life that you shared with your twin. Please remember these past life experiences are coming from your soul history within the Akashic Records. The rules still apply, even if you are asleep.

You should set an intention prior to going to sleep, but do not open the Records and leave them open. The soul has its own way of accessing the Akashic Records while you sleep. There is no need to consciously open them and leave them open all night. You likely wouldn't sleep much anyway because of the Akashic energy.

Allow yourself to have the experience in your dreams, and then allow yourself to have total recall. This is part of your intention because you are giving your conscious brain permission to remember your dream experiences. Your brain may not understand everything it witnessed, but by allowing the experience to happen and setting an intention to remember it, you've given your brain a job and a purpose in this process. Remember, things tend to work a bit easier when you give your rational-thinking, analytical brain a job to do that assists with the process.

The second your eyes open, grab your journal and write. It doesn't matter how little or how much, as long you write. I often set my alarm for an earlier time just so I'll have time to write, so that could be an option. I would give yourself time to adjust to this pattern, that is if you don't already keep a dream journal of any kind.

If you experience something in your dreams that you disagree with or don't resonate with, you can always reach out for assistance on how to deal with it. It is likely that the reason these things came up in your dream is because you're facing or dealing with something similar now. It could also be likely that, by experiencing this past life, your soul demonstrated to you just exactly how far you've come on the path to soul evolution.

For example, the very first past life regression session I did was in a group setting with Dr. Brian Weiss. I set my intention to have a regression back to a life with my twin flame as a means of continuing my cycle of proof. What came out of the session was an experience that shook me to my core. In the past life I experienced, I was a vicious but revered warrior who was merciless when it came to his enemies, whether it was during battle or even at his homes. It was so far from the peace-loving, laid-back, lightworker that I am now that I wasn't sure it could be real, nor did I have any idea of how to process this experience at all. I also learned that Chico was my older brother in that existence, and he was murdered by my enemies, which was part of the reason that this warrior was so ruthless.

I immediately began research on the time period, trying to see what I could discover. The more that I learned, the less I understood it. At least until a mentor said to me, "Yeah, okay, so all that happened way back centuries ago. Look how far you've come! Look how many lessons you have had to learn to be who you are now! Besides, in historical context, this guy's actions were common. Past life regression is just that, it's past. The only thing it has to do with your present are the lessons through which your soul progresses."

Oh, and by the way, I should mention one more thing: this doesn't just count for past lives on Earth. There can be interplanetary lives, god/goddess lives, or lives in other galaxies, just to name a few. There could also be Atlantean, pre-Atlantean, or prehistoric existences on Earth. Don't discount anything you receive. The same signs would still apply here, although how do we truly know if they wear sneakers on Venus? Still, write everything down. Nothing will come to you that isn't important.

The things that I experienced in past lives usually had some bearing or connection to something that was going on in the present time. They usually presented a root cause for whatever feelings I had or actions I did.

Past Lives in the Akashic Records

There are several ways to experience past lives: in dreams, in hypnosis, and in past life regression. There is also a direct way to access this information in the Records.

Just like the twin flame journey, we can open the Akashic Records with a specific intention that will allow us to experience a past life. You should, by now, have an idea of the unbreakable cord that connects you with your twin. The cord for me and Chico is purple, but perhaps you experienced a different color in meditation. That's okay. There is no wrong or right color, there is only the color of you and your twin.

When you open the Records and connect with your soul energy, this specific intention will allow you to not only experience what your life was like and your role in it, but you will also be able to gain an understanding of your twin's life in the same existence. You will be able to ascertain if they incarnated into an existence at the same time, as well as whether you knew one another if you were both incarnate.

This is not a question-and-answer session within the Records. Just like the twin flame journey, this is an experience to be received. There will be plenty of information within your past life experience to question and learn more about in a separate session. Just be sure to record everything that you see, feel, hear, experience, and understand and be open to receive.

Opening the Records

Blessed Agents of Light,

Thank you for your loving presence. I come to you with an open heart and an open mind that are both ready to receive your guidance as I partake on this journey. It is my intention to learn about and experience a previous incarnation in the timeline of my soul. I also intend to understand the role my divine counterpart played in this previous lifetime. I wish to see, feel, know, experience, and understand this previous existence through your eyes in all ways that are for my best and highest good. Please direct me to my soul's energy within your loving light, to a previous existence that has a specific connection to my current one and show me that connection. I ask for your assistance and wisdom in service of myself, (insert full legal name).

It is so, and so it is. Amen.

The Records are now open.

Closing the Records

Blessed Agents of Light,

Thank you for your guidance, assistance, and your wisdom. I am in gratitude for all that I have received. Please allow me to recall all that I have experienced once I have departed from your light.

It is so and so it is. Amen.

The Records are now closed.

———

It is incredibly important to just allow yourself to experience whatever comes, and trust that you haven't experienced it for any other reason other than it's in your best interest. As I said, sometimes we do experience unpleasant things that occurred in past lives. Just remember, these things are in the past and you witnessed them again because they help explain something going on in your current life. You may, for example, discover that the reason you don't like to wear anything around your neck, like a turtleneck sweater or a choker necklace, is because you were hung in a previous existence. You could also not like being in cold or deep water because you passed away when the *R.M.S. Titanic* sank in 1912.

These things are possible to uncover in past life experiences. It is also possible to learn that your twin lived a life in Ireland and helped build the *Titanic*. It's also possible to learn that the reason you have a connection to a specific historical time period in your current existence is because you lived a past life in that time period. You could be a Civil War buff in the present day, for example, because you experienced it first-hand as a soldier in 1864.

This is what makes it important to remain open to whatever comes. You just never know what may be explained. One more example from myself and Chico: we were both writers in a previous life. He was a poet, and I wrote a scary novel. I hadn't read any of this work prior to learning about this existence, so it was fascinating to learn of our literary prowess. Before you ask, I own copies of the poetry and the novel. They are in my library. I would never have learned about this, and been able to locate these texts, if I rejected the past life experience. This is the reason that I encourage you to reject nothing.

Chapter 8
Divination

Divination is the art of seeking and gaining knowledge via unusual, metaphysical, or supernatural means. This word generally has a negative connotation attached to it because it is most often used to describe a method to obtain information about the future. This isn't correct. There is no way to be able to ascertain absolute information about the future because we all have free will. Even the Akashic Records, the place that houses the history of your soul, cannot predict the future. At best, divination will provide you with information about situations that may occur if you do not change your actions, your words, or your will.

There are many methods that fall under the divination umbrella. We will discuss a few of them within this chapter, which you may use to help you prove the relationship, to connect with your twin, and to assist you on your spiritual path. Get ready to dive in because there's quite a bit in this chapter. I will provide you with a little background about them, and a direct way to utilize each of these methods to connect with your twin flame.

Method One: Signs

Designate a sign meant to symbolize your twin flame and then look for the acknowledgements that will come. This works with both incarnate and discarnate twins. If you ask for the number 444 to show up as a sign from your twin, you will receive it. You must remember, even if you do not know one another and you are both incarnate on Earth, you are always connected. Your twin will provide the signs you asked for even if they may not be consciously aware of it.

The operational theory for this method is simple: when you ask for specific signs with the intention to receive them only from your twin, they will be received from your twin. The caveat that I add here is that, when a person is starting out on their journey, whether it's their spiritual path or the path to connecting with their twin flame, it is often a lack of self-confidence and self-trust that prevents people from moving forward: "Well, how can I trust myself with this? I'm new to all of this. My experiences cannot be real." Trust me, I've said all these phrases and more (and usually with expletives). To those of you who may believe this way I say: give yourself a break. This isn't an easy path, and you cannot be expected to just trust everything right off the bat.

I must also say that receiving signs from your twin is a pretty good way to start to claim that self-confidence and self-trust. You must allow yourself to believe what you receive is real. This method of proving the relationship is a fun one to start off with. Make sure to keep track of whatever signs that you ask for and when you receive them. Trust me, validation is loads of fun.

This method requires asking your twin to validate your connection by giving you specific signs. You can do this by simply asking out loud. Those on the Other Side, including your discarnate twin flame, will hear you and answer. For those twins who are both incarnate, this method can also work for you. This requires a connection with your twin's higher-self to ask for the signs. Twin flames will always validate their connection to one another.

So, if you have done all this work up until now, then you have likely been able to establish a common theme for signs between yourself and your twin. Chico and I have several: the number 333, hearts, circles, and the number one, just to name a few. To test this theory, I decided to pick a couple of these and slam them together for specific signs. Below are the steps that I followed to test this method.

1. Pick a specific sign: Don't just say, "Hey, if you're my twin, give me a sign." There is no way to validate it, unless you see the words I AM YOUR TWIN FLAME painted on a billboard on the side of the highway. That would be totally amazing. You should ask for something specific, though. Choose something that will be meaningful only to you and your twin.

   I chose a couple of different signs: circles and hearts. The first sign had to be a circle and the second sign had to be a heart. It doesn't matter what the sign is that you choose, just so long as it's used with the intention that you only receive it from your twin.

2. Set an intention: It doesn't matter if your twin is on this plane or on the Other Side. When you set your intention to communicate with your twin, you are doing so with the understanding that if your twin is also incarnate, you are connecting with their higher-self. Here is the intention that I used, including my specific request:

I intend to use the following signs to not only connect with my twin flame—regardless of where their soul is located—but to assist in proving the twin flame relationship. When these signs are received, I will know beyond the shadow of a doubt that I have received them from my twin flame. Please allow this knowledge and connection from my soul and higher-self to the soul and higher-self of my twin flame. The first sign I wish to receive is a copper circle. I would like to receive it first thing in the morning and I would like to be able to carry it with me. The second sign I wish to receive is a heart. This heart should be either the color white or royal blue. I would like to be able to receive this in a moment when I really need it. I would like to be able to carry it with me. I am in gratitude. It is so, and so it is. Amen.

3. Look for the signs: I asked for two very specific signs. I did this because I had no doubt that I would receive them in the way that I asked for them. If you are just starting out on this twin flame path, I would recommend just picking one very specific sign and then asking for it in as many ways as you can possibly think of.

4. Record the results: You always want to record what you receive. The reason we want to save this information is because it is validation of the connection and relationship.

Here is what I received in answer to my request. First thing you should know is that Chico excels at giving signs, especially when I challenge him with uber-specific ones. Second thing: your results could be very similar because the more specific you are in your intention and requests, the more you give your twin to work with. Sometimes they're literal, other times they can be creative. Be sure to be open to receive whatever comes. Let's start with the results for the first sign I asked my twin to send to me.

I started this little experiment for research on April 23, 2018. I set my intention the night before and then went to sleep. I got up at my normal time, got ready for work, and then realized that I needed to stop at the gas station first thing that morning. I pulled into a parking place in front of the building, opened the door and got out. I looked down, and on the ground was a penny right beside my car door. Chico sends me pennies quite often, so this wasn't really a surprise. I asked for a copper circle to be received first thing in the morning and I'd like to be able to carry it with me. I received a copper penny lying on the ground at about 6:15 a.m. I picked it up and placed it in my car. Usually, I take a photograph of every sign I receive in the place and way that I receive it before I touch it. Since I was still half-asleep, I just picked it up and put it in my car, with a big smile on my face and then I thanked him. It's important to be in gratitude whenever you receive a sign from spirit and your twin. Chances are likely that they've worked pretty hard to ensure you receive that sign.

The second sign came April 30, 2018, at a time when I really wasn't looking for it and I'd pretty much forgotten that I was supposed to be on the lookout for signs so we could complete our research for this method. I was on my way home from work when my gas light came on. I intended to stop at my usual place, but I didn't think that the car could last that long. So, I pulled into the first gas station I saw. This just goes to show that I also should've been paying attention to my gas gauge.

Here is where it really gets awesome, though, so it turned out to be a good thing that I nearly ran out of gas. I don't remember what pump number I pulled up to, but the moment I opened my door to get out, I had to smile. My second sign was right there on the ground. Not only did I get a white heart, but I also got a white circle. Circles symbolize the oneness of us all, but also for twin flames it can symbolize the oneness of the relationship.

Both would have been kept except the white heart looked like it was chewed bubble gum and the white circle was plastic that had teeth marks on it (yeah, I got close enough to inspect it). I settled for just snapping a photo.

This was a pretty good method; I enjoyed working through it. It is just another piece of the larger twin flame puzzle. Your twin flame will always validate themselves to you, no matter what plane they're on.

Method Two: Mediumship

Mediumship is the act of communication with those who have transitioned from this life to the Other Side. We've already established that you can connect with your twin's higher-self, and this works for incarnate twins. When it comes to discarnate twins, it is an option to utilize mediumship to actively communicate with one another.

Before we go any further, let me be clear: I'm not saying that you should learn how to communicate with those on the Other Side just so you can talk to your discarnate twin flame. You can speak directly to each other within the Akashic Records, as previously discussed. Communication for those on both sides of the veil is a sacred privilege. Eventually, no matter the reason you get into learning about it, you'll end up assisting others as well as yourself. It's just inevitable. I got in to learning about mediumship because I wanted to find a way to shut Chico up! I never did find that way. Instead, I took many classes and became a certified psychic medium. It is the natural evolution when you work with those on the Other Side.

Spirit communication is about building bridges, bringing love, and healing, and proving the continuity of life beyond a shadow of a doubt. It is not about learning how to speak with your discarnate twin flame.

Self-Mediumship

There are ways to be able to communicate with your twin that fall under the mediumship category, and they're not as difficult as you may think. The methods that follow are examples of what I like to call "self-mediumship." This means that you learn how to rely on and trust in your own feelings, experiences, and abilities. In doing so, you also gather evidence that will help explain and define your relationship.

You can gain information about their previous existence via divination tools, such as a pendulum. Remember, if you can prove the twin flame relationship on Earth, then you have proven it period. The key is simple: be curious and learn. There is nothing to fear, especially when trying to communicate with the other part of your divine soul.

The best way to utilize this method to communicate with your twin is by using a divination tool, such as a pendulum or a spirit board. These two forms of communication seem to have a bad reputation, thanks to improper use in films and on TV, so let's discuss what they are and how to use them properly.

Pendulums

A pendulum is a device that has a crystal or a stone at the end of it. This is then attached to a long chain. When used properly, you can use this tool to communicate with those on the Other Side, and with the higher-self of those who are incarnate.

There are many different types of pendulums, including ones made specifically for communication, but you can also use other items. I have used a necklace with a weighted charm on it, for example, or a keychain with keys on it. The point of a pendulum is that it allows spirit to use their energy to move it to answer your questions.

You can utilize this to communicate with your twin, whether they are incarnate or discarnate. I recommend that you pick one specific pendulum and set the intention that its only use will be to communicate with your twin flame. Select your pendulum and then you'll want to clear it of any other energy. You can clear your pendulum using one of the following methods:

- Leave your pendulum on a windowsill overnight and allow the energy of the moon to clear it.

- Hold your pendulum in your left hand and pull down universal white light in through the top of your head, through your body, and into the pendulum to clear it.
- Hold your pendulum in your left hand and set the intention that universal white light will come in through your crown chakra, through your body, and fill up your lungs. Then blow the white light into your pendulum.

The pendulum should be cleared because, well, any number of others could have held it. We leave our energy imprint on things we encounter every day, and if someone else has tried to use the pendulum to communicate with spirit or if the pendulum has been used for other things, then there will be a whole lot of extra energy attached to it.

Once cleared, you will need to attune the pendulum to your energy. To do this, simply hold it in your right hand and set the intention that your energy will fill the pendulum and that it will be divinely protected.

After you have charged the pendulum with your energy, you can ask for permission to attune it to your twin's energy. If your twin is on the Other Side, this is relatively easy: just ask them to infuse the pendulum with their energy. Hold the pendulum in your right hand and allow your twin's energy to utilize your arm and hand to infuse the pendulum with their energy. If your twin is incarnate, simply use this intention:

I now ask for permission from my twin flame's higher-self to infuse their energy into this pendulum, mixing with my own.

There's no difference in how your energies will feel, though a discarnate twin's energy might feel a little bit tingly. It's that tingling sensation you get after your foot falls asleep and it finally wakes up. This occurs with discarnate energy because it flows at a much higher vibration than that of the physical body. Otherwise, there is really no difference in energy because it comes from the same source and carries the same spiritual DNA.

When doing any kind of spirit communication (and this includes if your twin is incarnate because you're communicating with their higher-self), you must always approach it with your own energy calm, clear, open, and ready. In other words, don't try to communicate if you are sad or angry or if you cannot clear your own energy. Your compromised energy will affect what you receive, and your ability to even connect to your twin.

It's the basic principle of the law of attraction: what you put out you will receive back. So, if you pick up your pendulum and try to communicate while you are angry, for example, you will receive anger in return. And nine times out of ten, that anger won't come from the soul with whom you intended to communicate. It will come from a lower energy being instead. Remember, like attracts like. Be of the light, work with the light.

Using a Pendulum

Using your pendulum is easy, but there is a proper method you should follow. When you do not utilize the pendulum properly, it really becomes a worthless tool. You can't receive information properly if you are not properly connected. This is the method for using your pendulum to connect with your twin flame.

First, clear your energy by deep breathing, grounding, and bringing in the universal white light. Once cleared, you can pick up your pendulum, but not before.

Next, call in your spiritual team. This team will consist of your guides, angels, loved ones and so many others. It doesn't matter whether you know who they are or not, they're there to assist both sides with communication. I also personally include Jesus when I call in my team.

Here is the full intention that I use:

I intend to utilize this session to communicate with my twin flame. I ask that all my guides, angels, loved ones, and Master Jesus surround and light the way for clear communication between me and my twin flame. Allow the protective energy of Archangel Michael to envelop this communication, our energy, this space, and this connection. Let none other than whom I have intended come forth to communicate. I am open to receive. It is so and so it is. Amen.

Most pendulums have something on the end of the chain to hold onto. Gently grasp it with your thumb and index finger. Don't hold it too tightly, okay, you want it to be able to flow with the energy from spirit. Make sure to hold the pendulum with your dominant hand and extend your arm out away from your body.

Ask the pendulum to show you movement for a "yes" answer. "Please show me yes."

Ask the pendulum to show you movement for a "no" answer. "Please show me no."

Now, ask the pendulum three test questions and note the answers you receive. If the answers are correct, continue. If the answers are incorrect, go back to the first step and clear your energy again. And then reset your intentions.

Conduct your session by asking questions. This is a bit like playing spiritual Jeopardy, except that instead of the answers being in the form of a question, the answers can only be "yes" or "no." (Well, at least at first. The more you practice, the more you will be able to decipher beyond yes or no.)

For example, you may ask your twin: "Is your birthday in April?" And the pendulum will indicate "No" as an answer from your twin.

"Okay, is your birthday before April?" The pendulum indicates that your twin answered "Yes." And then you can ask in which month, January, February, or March, that their birthday appears.

Once you decide to end your session, be sure to thank your twin and your spiritual team. And then ask your team to help close the session.

Do not just lay your pendulum down without closing the session. It's exactly like leaving your car window open during a rainstorm, rain still flows into the car. Energy is still flowing within, around, and through that active pendulum.

Here is the full intention that I use to close the session:

I intend that this pendulum session is now closed. I would like to thank my twin flame and I release your energy. Please return home. Archangel Michael, please clear all energy that is attached to this pendulum at this time and spin the pendulum in a circle to let me know when you're finished. I am in gratitude. It is so and so it is. Amen.

Closing the session will include clearing your pendulum of energy. This simply indicates a removal of any extra energy left by your spiritual team while they were helping during the session.

Here's a tip: you can also open the Akashic Records before you begin your pendulum session and use it to get answers in the Records. You still follow the steps I've outlined here but open the Records first by using the regular intention prayer. It's a very high vibration and you'll get an amazing energetic response.

Spirit Boards

The same rule holds true for a spirit board: you must always approach it with your own energy calm, clear, open, and ready. Do not attempt to communicate using a spirit board if you have not cleared your own energy and are not coming from an objective place of love. Remember: like attracts like. If you come in with anger, that's what you'll receive in return, regardless of how many times you call in your spiritual team for guidance and protection.

Most of the time, whenever we witness a spirit board (also called a Ouija board) being utilized on television and in movies, there is no proper method being used at all (or at least one isn't shown). It is possible to access those not in the light on the Other Side by using divination tools improperly, and this is most common when there is no proper method in place to help use and govern the tools.

A spirit board, regardless of if you buy it from a store or create it yourself, must be cleared of all energy. The same principle applies here as it did for the pendulum: you don't know how many other people have left their energy imprint on it prior to you receiving it. If you created your board, either out of paper or some other method, the board should still be cleared. You cannot be sure that you were in the best frame of mind or that your energy was calm when it was created. You can use any of the following to clear your spirit board.

Like the pendulum, you can place your board either on your windowsill or outside in a safe place where it cannot be damaged and someone else cannot touch it. The moon's energy will ensure that your board is clear and ready for use.

You can create a mixture of sea salt (or kosher salt) and cool water (1/3 cup of water, 1 teaspoon of sea salt), spray it on a clean cloth or a paper towel, and wash the board. Do not drown the board with the mixture, it isn't necessary. Simply spray the cloth and wipe the board. The salt will clear the energy. I personally use salt from the Dead Sea.

Ground and center yourself, and then intend that the universal white light enter your body through your crown chakra. Then, place your hands on the center of the board and intend that the white light clear the board from corner to corner, front and back.

Using a Spirit Board

Spirit boards have a very bad reputation, thanks to Hollywood, but using a spirit board is truly easy and there's nothing to fear, provided there is a proper method being used.

First, clear your energy by deep breathing, grounding, and bringing in the universal white light. Once you have done this, then you may handle or touch the spirit board. Do not do so before you have cleared your energy.

Next, call in your spiritual team. I include Jesus in this request.

I also surround myself, my energy, my twin and his energy, the space I'm located in, and the entire energy of the session with the protective energy of the archangel of protection, Michael.

This is my entire intention that I use for each session:

I intend that this session will be used to communicate with my twin flame. I ask that all my guides, angels, loved ones, and Master Jesus surround and light the way for clear communication between me and my twin flame. I intend that this session, the energies of myself, my twin, my spiritual team, and this space be divinely protected and covered with the mighty energy of Archangel Michael. Let none other than whom I have intended and asked for enter this session. Nothing can penetrate my angelic protection. It is so and so it is. Amen.

You can find something that works for you, of course, but the point is that I call in all angels when I work with a spirit board just to ensure that everything is divinely protected and for everyone's best and highest good.

If you are communicating in the session alone: place your index fingers from both hands lightly onto the planchette. You can then ask for your twin to bring their energy forward and communicate. Do not move your fingers off the planchette, and don't press too hard. The energy needs to be able to flow freely.

Here's a tip: you can also use a pendulum to swing over the appropriate letters. If you choose to work in this way, please also follow the process for preparing your pendulum.

Start off with easier questions at first. You don't want to overwhelm yourself or your twin."Please tell me the first letter of your first name. Okay, now spell the rest of your name."

Here's another tip: try to audio record your session. You should not move your fingers off the planchette (or pendulum;

whichever you decide to use), so you cannot write any information down that you receive. You can try to remember it all, but when you get on a roll during your session, you'll do well to remember what questions you asked let alone the answers you received.

Once you decide to end your session, be sure to thank your twin and your spiritual team, including Archangel Michael. Don't just put your board away and think that's the end. It is still an open conduit for communication until you close the session and clear the energies from it. Ask your team to help close the session.

Close your intention:

I intend that this session is now closed. I would like to thank my twin flame and I release your energy. Please return home. Archangel Michael, please clear all energy that is attached to this spirit board at this time. I trust that you have done so. Thank you for your assistance. I am in gratitude. It is so and so it is. Amen.

Just to ensure that everyone's energy is cleared from the board, especially if I conduct it with several other people, I again clear the board by using the saltwater mixture. I dry it off and then put it away, I do not let it air dry.

When I first used a spirit board to try and communicate with Chico, he wasn't a big fan. He would rather that I would try to speak with him using my own mediumistic abilities, rather than to rely on the spirit board. This was part of my personal lessons, and it was designed to help me open to spirit much more and experience them.

I mention it to illustrate something important: your twin knows what vibes with you and what doesn't. If you give the spirit board a try and have little or no success, don't despair. It simply means that the spirit board wasn't the best way to communicate with your twin. I usually say that if you try it three times and there isn't much success, then it might be best to move away from the spirit board, at least for a little while. There might be a better avenue for your twin to communicate with you.

Keep in mind that you can use a spirit board to communicate with both incarnate and discarnate twin flames. If they're on the Other Side, then you simply bring their energy in for the session, but if they are incarnate on Earth then you would need permission to communicate with your twin's higher-self.

Mediums and Twin Flames

This section is truly more informative than anything. It's important to understand how to enter a reading with a medium. People will often seek help from a medium to help communicate with their twin on the Other Side. I have been known to seek sessions with other mediums just to give Chico the opportunity to speak through them if he was so inclined. Granted, my readings with others weren't always centered around validating my relationship. My other loved ones, guides, angels, and others would come through and provide loving messages, but every now and then, Chico would show up and give so many intricate details through the medium that his presence was undeniable. All those moments are recorded as not only spirit communication in my diaries, but also as validation of the relationship. No matter what the message, Chico would always throw direct validation into the reading that centered around our twin flame connection.

There is nothing wrong with considering this kind of assistance to validate your relationship. You just need make sure you set your intention first because your twin knows what you need. You also must understand the guidelines. Yep, no matter who you have a mediumship reading with, there should be guidelines. If there aren't, don't stay. Seriously, get up and leave right away.

First, other than perhaps your name, do not give the medium any information. If you do, your validation goes out the window. For example, do not walk into a mediumship reading and say this:

"Hi, my name is Leslie and I think that Abraham Lincoln is my twin flame because I have had all of these experiences and read all of these books and I want you to tell me that I'm right."

You've already given the medium way too much information. If they're unscrupulous and ego driven, the medium might answer with something like:

"Oh, of course he is! I can totally see the similarities between the two of you now! I mean, your first name and his last name begin with the same letter! It's totally amazing!"

I would never do that. I would stop you from saying anything past telling me your name. A medium cannot help or hope to prove the twin flame relationship if you've already given them all the information they need. Don't feed the medium information. That isn't your job. Your job is to receive information.

I once was given permission to listen to a recording of what a friend of mine thought was a validation reading of her idea of her twin flame. This reading was utterly disheartening to me. There was my friend, asking a steady stream of questions, but instead of saying something along the lines of, "I really just want to know more about my twin flame" she gave his name, explained the premise of why she believed this person was her twin and waited for the validation in response.

I wasn't surprised to hear the medium's answer: "Yes, of course you are correct."

I stopped listening after that. It didn't take a psychic to predict how it turned out.

The only way to get true validation from a medium is to let your twin on the Other Side give the information. If there is a real, true connection, your twin will always validate it. We know that twin flames are always connected no matter what, so that bond will always be validated. The best way to walk into a reading with a medium is this:

"Hi! My name is Leslie and I'm open to receive."

Set your intention first and ask your twin to come in during the session. You can ask out loud, or in your mind, or write it on paper. No matter how you ask, your twin will understand you. Keep in mind that the medium cannot guarantee who will or will not come through to them. Spirit on the Other Side has control over that. Sometimes your twin might think that there's a different medium with other specialties that may be a better fit for the kind of validation that they want to give to you. Ask your twin to lead you to the right medium, there's nothing wrong with that.

This also works for receiving validation for an incarnated twin flame by asking your twin's higher-self to allow a connection with the medium. The higher-self is connected to the divine through the soul, so a medium can connect on a psychic level. The difference between a psychic level and a mediumship level is simple: it's just a different kind of energy.

Psychic energy connects with your aura and the higher-self. This is the only energy that a psychic can connect with. Mediumship energy is connecting directly to those on the Other Side. All mediums are psychic but not all psychics are mediums. A medium can also connect to these energies of the aura and the higher-self, but they get their information by connecting with spirit on the Other Side. When seeking validation about the twin flame relationship from others, I would recommend starting with a medium.

A Little Validation of My Own

I had so many readings during which I received messages and validation from Chico that there is no possible way I could list all of it. I have it saved, mostly in written form and in photographs. The most profound validation I have received, however, came at a time when I truly began to doubt everything I'd learned and experienced. I was on the verge of getting rid of all the research I'd done, and just moving on and forgetting all about Chico. I received the following message at an event on March 14, 2015: "You are the other part of me—and now LIVE YOUR LIFE."

This medium, Roland Comtois, knew nothing about me, and yet this was the written message he channeled for me from Chico. You'll also notice that the last three words are all in capital letters: "LIVE YOUR LIFE." I always thought that was an interesting thing for Chico to say (and for the medium to channel from him). I believed it was meant as a pick-me-up, as though he were saying, "Stop letting stuff get you down and get out there and live." Over time, my opinion evolved to maybe he was saying, "Stop wasting time proving this whole twin flame thing. We are who we are so believe it and move on." I believe this to partially still be true, but I also found other things that simultaneously shocked and delighted me.

Your twin will always validate a true connection and relationship in every possible way. Chico gave me validation on this channeled paper, and it took almost five years for me to notice. I found writing from when Chico was alive where his signature was preceded by the words "LIVE ON" in all capital letters. The word "LIVE" looked nearly identical to the one in my channeled message. It took my breath away when I discovered this. This indicated to me that at least this part of Roland's handwritten message may be in Chico's handwriting instead of his. Some of the other things I have seen from Chico while he was on Earth indicate that this may be true, mostly because the handwriting looks so similar that it's unmistakable.

Maybe your validation might not be as bold or as dramatic as Chico's, because believe me sometimes he must get right in my face with messages and validation. It just proves that a true relationship will always be validated and proven, no matter what plane they are on.

The following methods may be shorter in description, but they are equally as useful as the first two. The theme for all of them is simple: just relax and allow. There is a lot of energetic work here, and it is important to ground your physical self and then raise your vibration so that you may be open to working with your twin. These methods will work with both discarnate and incarnate twins, though for incarnate twins you are seeking permission to work with their higher-self. Always remember to set your intention before you try out each method, and to close your session.

Method Three: Automatic Writing

This is the act of channeling words or thoughts from your twin (or from those on the Other Side in general) either through writing by hand or via typing on the computer. Sometimes you may even be able to channel words written in their handwriting, not yours. This is most effective for the twins while the Akashic Records are open, and you set a specific intention to channel from your twin.

The key to this method is to relax and allow. The sensation of either your discarnate twin or your incarnate twin's higher self can feel strange at first. You are essentially giving your twin permission to use your hand to write, or your fingers to type on a keyboard. My hand gets that tingly feeling like it does with the pendulum whenever Chico writes through me. This amazing method is another direct form of communication between yourself and your twin.

There is equal preparation for this method in that your energy cannot be compromised in any way. It's essential to remember that like attracts like, and if you approach this method with uncalm energy then that is what you will receive in return, regardless of who you invoke in your intention. Take a few minutes before your session to sit quietly, breathe deeply, and go through the process of clearing your energy, grounding yourself, and raising your vibration. You will also need to decide whether you need to sit in front of a keyboard or if you need paper and a pen. I usually write with one specific pen in a notebook whenever I channel from Chico.

It is important to set your intention. I will give you the two that I use, both within and outside of the Akashic Records.

This is the one I use for sessions outside of the Akashic Records:

My dear twin flame, I intend that this session be utilized as a way for your words, thoughts, ideas, and inspiration to be expressed. I give you permission to use my energy, my thoughts, my hearing, and other necessary elements of my physicality, to express yourself. I call in our guides, loved ones, angels, Master Jesus, and Archangel Michael to surround, protect, and guide this session. I am open to receive the energy of my divine counterpart. It is so and so it is. Amen.

Take a deep breath and relax. You can even close your eyes if you wish. You will know when the session begins. For me, I feel the tingly sensation in my hand and then my hand just starts moving.

You can prepare questions beforehand or you can allow your twin to just write freely. It's your choice.

Here's a tip: your twin will never get tired of writing to you. Set a time limit via an alarm. You can start off with shorter sessions of five minutes and then work your way upward. Your twin is using your energy and your body to assist them, so it's important you don't get tired out.

When you decide to end the session, do not just put your pen down. If you are typing, do not just put the keyboard away. These are still open vessels for communication. The energy is still present. You must close the session properly. Here is my closing intention:

My dear twin flame, thank you for your time, your words, and your love. I now release your energy from this session. Please return home. I ask that Archangel Michael remove all energy from this tool and this session. I trust that this is done. Thank you for your assistance. It is so and so it is. Amen.

When it comes to the Akashic Records, we now know that there must be a specific intention prior to opening them. You can set specific intentions to learn so many different things within the Records. It is fascinating what you can learn. Since you can also communicate directly with your twin within the Records, it's important to have as many ways as possible to facilitate that connection. Here are the opening and closing prayers that I use when it comes to automatic writing from Chico in the Akashic Records.

Opening the Records

Blessed Agents of Light,

Thank you for your loving presence. I come to you with an open heart and an open mind that are both ready to receive your guidance. I wish to see, feel, know, understand, and experience the divine connection with the other half of my soul within the light of your guidance. I wish to share and receive written communication (or electronic communication) with my divine counterpart. I ask for your assistance and wisdom in service of myself, _____ (insert your current full legal name here).

It is so, and so it is. Amen.

The Records are now open.

Closing the Records

Blessed Agents of Light,

Thank you for your guidance, and your wisdom. Thank you for allowing me to experience this divine partnership through your eyes without judgment or fear. Thank you for sharing your love. I am in gratitude for all that I have received.

It is so and so it is. Amen.

The Records are now closed.

Method Four: Psychometry

Psychometry is the name of the metaphysical method that is used to connect with someone's energy via an object or a photograph. This can also include videos of someone. Everything we touch or carry with us leaves an energy imprint, including photos of us. When we connect with the energy of another we can connect with their soul.

If you have an item that belonged to or an image of someone that you believe is your twin, you can hold that item or image and then take it with you on the twin flame journey. If it is something that you cannot hold, carry the impression of it with you in your mind and complete the twin flame journey. If this item belonged to your twin, or if this is a photograph of your twin, you will be able to connect with it through the umbilical-like cord that connects you and your twin throughout all space and time forever.

You can also use a photograph, an item, or a video to connect with your twin outside of the twin flame journey. One of the ways to determine your connection to your twin is by your twin flame cord, so in your intention you can request to see, feel, know, understand, or experience your cord as it is attached to the item, video, or photograph. This cord will always be represented for a true and valid relationship.

Remember to clear your energy first and ensure its calm and uncompromised. Here is the intention that I use:

I intend that this object, photograph, or video be utilized as a connection to my twin flame. If this is a true, valid, and right connection, please allow me to experience, see, feel, or understand the presence of the unique and unbreakable cord that exists between my divine counterpart and myself. It cannot be replicated in any way, other than to establish and prove the twin flame connection. It is so and so it is. Amen.

I have one item in my possession that belonged to Chico on Earth. I received it before I learned about our unbreakable cord, though I immediately felt his energy on it the moment I touched it. This item has his thumbprints and his signature on it, so even after nearly three decades, his energy was still tangible.

I recently went back to this item and set my intention to see our cord attached to it. I experienced with my clairvoyance an awesome and equally funny sight. The cord wasn't just attached to this item, it was wrapped around it so tightly that it looked bent. I instinctively knew that this was Chico's usual in-your-face approach to revealing our cord.

Method Five: Tarot and Oracle Cards

These decks of cards are a tool of divination usually used to acquire information from your higher-self and soul. Tarot cards are mainly used to connect with the higher-self in a psychic reading. Oracle cards are also used in the same way, however many oracle decks can also be used to connect with those on the Other Side and in the higher realms, such as angels and archangels. There are even specific decks that focus primarily on the twin flame connection.

When I tried out this method, I bought a deck and before I even opened it, I set the intention that I would only use this deck to communicate with my twin. I reset that intention every single time I use the deck, too, and call in my spiritual team for guidance, assistance, and protection during each session.

There's a little bit of preparation that you should do beforehand, though. First, clear your energy. There are easily thirty other people who touched these cards before you did, even if they're brand new in plastic, so it's important to clear the cards. You can use the same methods to clear the cards that you used for the pendulum:

- Leave your deck on a windowsill overnight and allow the energy of the moon to clear it.
- Hold your deck in your left hand and pull down universal white light in through the top of your head, through your body, and into the deck to clear it.
- Hold your deck in your left hand and set the intention that universal white light will come in through your crown chakra, through your body, and fill up your lungs. Then blow the white light into your deck.
- You can also hold the deck in your left hand and knock three times with your right. Knocking the top card three times clears away energy, which makes room for your energy.

Once cleared, you can infuse your energy into the deck by touching every card. This way you only allow specific energy, namely that of your twin, to fuse with your energy. You can use the deck as a means of divining information from your higher-self and your soul. In this way, this is another method that can be used to prove the relationship. You can also connect with the higher-self of your incarnate twin, too. It's important to remember these methods can work with twins who are on Earth and those who are on the Other Side.

Once you have properly prepared yourself and your deck, it's time to set your intention. The intention is simple but effective:

> *I intend that this deck be used for the specific purpose of communicating with the energy of my twin flame and their higher-self. I invoke all my guides, loved ones, Jesus, and Archangel Michael to govern this session and surround us with protective light. I invite my divine counterpart to share his energy in this deck of cards within this session. None other may enter or penetrate our sacred space. It is so and so it is. Amen.*

If your deck comes with an instruction booklet, I recommend that you read it once all the way through. Then do not use it anymore. Working with card decks is all about your feelings: How does this card make you feel? What do feel it's saying to you? Often, the feeling you receive from the cards may not exactly align with the original intention from the author of the deck. When this happens, the inclination to dismiss your own intuition is strong. Don't dismiss it. Your answer doesn't always come from a book. It will always come from your intuition, and your twin.

You can ask whatever questions you want during the session. There is no specific way to ask or form that the questions must be in. You only need to ask and receive the answer. When the session is over, please remember to close it. Your cards are still an open portal for energy to flow through them, so it's important that you close the session. You can use this simple intention:

I intend that this session is closed. I release the energy of my divine counterpart and their higher-self. Please return home. I ask that Archangel Michael clear this space of all other energy. It is so and so it is. Amen.

After you've closed your session, go back through the deck, and touch each card. This seals in your energy on a freshly cleared deck (courtesy of Archangel Michael).

You can also create your own cards based on the intention of using them only to communicate with your twin. You can use images or cut out words from a magazine, for example, that make sense to you. Then, you can paste them onto a card. In the beginning, I created a deck of cards using images from the internet that I glued onto card stock. I used images that I was guided to, and the first card was a photo of Chico. This helped to set the intention that this deck could only be used to communicate with him.

It's all up to you. The most important thing is to set the intention.

Method Six: Spirit Art

Spirit art is any kind of art that is created by or divined from those on the Other Side. I usually break this category down into two categories: spirit drawing and "done by spirit." Let's discuss "done by spirit" first.

Done by Spirit

You must remember that all things are created from energy. Even if those on the Other Side have no physical body anymore, that does not mean they cannot create a painting or inspire a musical melody. They absolutely can. The lack of a physical body makes it easier because there are no limitations. They can draw, paint, color, sing, or do anything else they wish to do, regardless of whether they could do so when they were on Earth. I have seen slips of paper put into a basket and covered up. After a few minutes, they were uncovered to reveal different drawings done by those on the Other Side on each piece of paper. This is possible. It is also possible that if your twin is discarnate that you could ask them to create art for you.

I have some art that was done for me by Chico. It's unique because I tied some string on the end of a paintbrush and used it as a pendulum. He was able to move it around freely to create some interesting patterns. This is just one example of how spirit can create art. Don't limit yourself, be creative with your requests, your intentions, and your willingness to work with your discarnate twin.

The "done by spirit" category can also apply to incarnate twins as you would allow their higher-self to create the art. Often, the art could include guidance to images online or in magazines or books. This is because their higher-self is trying to communicate in ways that you'll both understand and aren't inclined to reject.

Spirit Drawing

This kind of art is usually done by a medium with the ability to draw images either of or from those on the Other Side with whom they communicate. This can work for both incarnate and discarnate twins, but my own experience leans toward this method being primarily beneficial for those who have transitioned to the Other Side.

If you are artistically inclined, you can open the Akashic Records and ask to connect with your twin to create art from what you see. It would be best to use the same intention you would use to open them for a question-and-answer session, with a couple of additions:

Opening the Records
Blessed Agents of Light,

Thank you for your loving presence. I come to you with an open heart and an open mind to seek answers to specific questions within your boundless energy. I wish to connect with the energy of my divine counterpart so that I may record their presence artistically. Thank you for your assistance. Please direct me to my soul energy within your guiding light. And please assist with the ability to artistically record my divine twin. I ask this in service of myself, _____ (insert your full current legal name here).

It is so and so it is. Amen.

The Records are now open.

Closing the Records
Blessed Agents of Light,

Thank you for your love, guidance, and wisdom. I am in gratitude for all that I have received.

It is so and so it is. Amen.

The Records are now closed.

During the session, you can ask your twin questions about their appearance on Earth in their most recent existence. You could ask questions such as:

- What was your skin tone?
- Will you show me what color eyes you had?
- Will you show me how tall you were?
- Will you show me the full length of your hair and its natural color?

These are just a few sample questions. The possibilities are endless. In the Records, you would see your twin through the eyes of the Agents of Light, so there would be clarity and purity to whatever you might witness.

Though I've done a few of these drawings myself (some of which were drawn before my mediumship abilities truly were in full swing), the first spirit drawing I received of Chico was done by an actual spirit artist. It was received about a year before I knew about our divine connection. The reading I received along with my drawing of Chico was full of so much validation about our experiences that it truly was the first piece of my puzzle, even though I did not realize that at the time. I just thought it was pretty darn cool to have a drawing of the guy I communicated with in my dreams every night. It was an essential piece of validation that proved he was real and not just a figment of my imagination.

Don't Forget About Your Cord!

You can also use the twin flame cord that connects you to memorialize your twin in art form. To do this, you would set your intention to connect in with your cord and utilize it to pull your twin close enough to experience a way to draw them (or create some other form of art).

The intention is almost the same as the one used with psychometry.

> *I intend that I will experience, see, feel or understand the presence of the unique and unbreakable cord that exists between my divine counterpart and myself. It cannot be replicated in any way, other than to establish and prove the twin flame connection. I further intend to draw my twin flame closer to me using the power of the shared spiritual DNA that created it. I call my soul twin to my side. It is so and so it is. Amen.*

When the session is over, please remember to close it. You can use this simple intention:

> *I intend that this session is closed. I release the energy of my divine counterpart. Please return home. I ask that Archangel Michael clear this space of all other energy. It is so and so it is. Amen.*

All these methods may also be used to assist with spirit communication in general, but if you're setting the specific intention that you wish to connect with your twin then you cannot get incorrect information.

You must also remember that once you open the door to communicating with those on the Other Side, that door will only open wider and wider. Please do not go into learning about communication with the understanding that the only person you will likely communicate with is your twin flame (or even your twin's higher-self). I began learning about those on the Other Side with the specific intention of finding a way to shut Chico up. Instead, I learned so much more. You never know what may happen so just be prepared.

Conclusion

We've discussed a lot of different methods of proving the twin flame relationship, and there are many more, which involve more soul work and further communication with your twin in other dimensions. I must admit that I was a bit overwhelmed when I sat down to go through my research and write about the methods I used to understand and prove my own twin flame relationship.

The amazing thing that I realized was that, despite my many protests and my fervent desire to disprove the entire concept, all the proof I needed came from my twin. He was there at every step, giving me what I needed, though I didn't realize it at the time. That's why I've repeatedly advised you to record and/or write everything down. What didn't make sense to me, or seemed extraneous at the time, turned out to be information that I needed. It just took me awhile to understand that.

So, we've walked through all these methods, and if you are anything like me, you have already gathered quite a lot of information. I have notebooks and binders full of information that I have collected over the better part of two decades. That's what happens when my Virgoan thirst for knowledge kicks in. I never know what I will end up with. I do know that quite a bit of the knowledge I have gained went into this book to assist you with learning about twin flames and proving the relationship.

After gaining this information and knowledge, I went back through all the methods and I realized that they all had a common theme. While processing and discovering this twin flame stuff, I gained a lot of insight and education that transformed me. I went from a complete skeptic who knew nothing about this whole twin flame gig, to someone who can write about, define, understand, and prove it. That's quite a change. I hope the same is true for you. I hope you can take the information and methods enclosed within this book and utilize it on your journey with your twin, as well as on your spiritual path of grace.

At the core of the twin flame relationship is that incredible vibration of universal divine love that creates the spiritual DNA. I don't know anyone who doesn't want to tap into that amazing love vibration, myself included. I realized that because of this understanding of this divine love at the core of our souls it wasn't important to me to keep proving the relationship anymore. I'd gone down the rabbit hole and realized that all there was to find was love.

There is the ultimate proof of the twin flame relationship. All parts of me morphed into this being that completely trusts myself and loves myself; and by doing so I have become more open to accepting my twin flame. The love at the core of our souls is equal and unmatched. Once self-love and trust exist and becomes incorruptible, then that truly paves the way for absolute validation of the twin flame relationship. No matter what you see, feel, hear, experience, or understand from others, there is nothing that will make more sense than the unbreakable connection between you and your divine counterpart.

In other words: it starts with you. It starts with your curiosity and your willingness to grow and learn and gain the necessary knowledge about twin flames.

Glossary

Air: The element that represents quickness, how animated you are, and the ability to apply energy in very diverse ways.

Akasha: A Sanskrit word that means "primary substance," out of which all things are formed. This is the root of the Akashic Records.

Akashic Records: The collective vibrational record of each individual soul and its journey.

Ancestry: The study of the direct lineage of ancestors using one's ethnicity.

Applying Aspect: In the astrological chart, this is when the degrees of two planets come closer to become more exact.

Aquarius: Sign of independence, improving society, and revolutionary ideals.

Aries: Sign of action and new beginnings.

Ascendant: Also called the rising sign, this is the first angle in the birth chart, which makes it one of four important angles in the birth chart. It is the cusp, or beginning, of the first house. It is also the indicator of how you say hello to the rest of the world.

Aspect: In the astrological chart, this is when two planets work in harmony or discord with one another through conjunction, opposition, square, trine, etc.

Astrology: The study of the movements and positions of the sun, the moon, planets, and stars through charts and how they influence human behavior.

Aura: The ever-changing flow of energy immediately around the physical body

Cancer: Sign of assertiveness and independence.

Capricorn: Sign of practicality, focus, sensibility, and hard work.

Cardinal: Quality that initiates change as part of the synastry of the astrological chart.

Chakras: The energetic system of the body that helps raise our spiritual energy vibration to reach the realms outside of the physical. Each chakra also assists the physical body with adapting to, releasing, and clearing out energy that affects the physical body.

Chaser: The twin who keeps the peace in the twin flame relationship. This role can change between the twins at any given time.

Clairalience: Clear smelling; this is the ability to smell things outside of the normal range of smell. It usually involves smells from spirit, such as their favorite flower or cologne. These smells do not originate from incarnate sources.

Clairaudience: Clear hearing; this is the ability to receive intuitive messages that doesn't necessarily use the physical ears. This is often through an inner voice or spirit.

Claircognizance: Clear knowing; this is the ability to know things that one would never, ever otherwise discern. It can be described as a "gut feeling" or "just knowing." Most file this clair as a part of clairsentience.

Clairgustance: Clear tasting; this is the ability to taste things without physically putting anything in your mouth. This usually comes from spirit to prove the continuity of life.

Clairsentience: Clear feeling; this is the ability to receive intuitive messages via feelings, emotions, or physical sensations.

Clairvoyance: Clear seeing; this is the ability to receive intuitive messages via a second sight. The physical eyes can perceive spirit or even a message from spirit, but most of the time messages come through as though you're watching a movie in your mind.

Conjunction: In astrology, this means unification and blending.

Cusp: The beginning of an angle in the astrological chart.

Descendant: One of four important angles in the birth chart, this is the angle opposite your ascendant. It is the seventh house cusp. This indicates your awareness of others and various aspects of relationships.

Discarnate: This is when a soul has not chosen to be born into a life and remains on the Other Side. This is usually so they can assist their incarnate twin.

Divine Feminine: The part of the spiritual DNA that is inherently feminine. This exists within each twin flame soul.

Divine Masculine: The part of the spiritual DNA that is inherently masculine. This exists within each twin flame soul.

Dream Visitation: This is the experience of spirit visiting you in your dreams. This is the easiest form of spirit communication.

Earth: The element that represents stoic reactions and the ability to apply energy with endurance.

Elements: There are four basic elements that, when applied to the astrological chart, represent basic traits.

Etheric: The is higher regions of space, the sky, the heavens. This is non-tangible space.

Etheric Body: The lowest layer of the human energy field that is in contact with the physical body to sustain and connect the physical body with higher bodies. The first layer of the aura.

Ethnicity: This is an ethnic group that shares common culture, nationality, religion, or language.

Fibonacci Sequence: This is a mathematical sequence associated with divine pattern and twin flames. It's the Golden Ratio that is reflected in architecture, octaves in music, roses, pinecones, and in spiral seashells. Written as a rule, the expression is xn=xn-1+xn-2.

Fire: The element that represents spontaneity, impulsiveness, and dedication.

Fixed: Quality that preserves change as part of the synastry of the astrological chart.

Gemini: Sign of communications and versatility.

Genealogy: This is the study of the line of continuous descent between ancestors.

Ghost: A discarnate soul who has transitioned from life on Earth but has not fully transcended to the Other Side. This is usually due to either a refusal to go or not having a sense that their lives have ended.

God: Your understanding of the omnipresent creator of all things.

Grounded: Your physical body, natural energy field, and aura are all rooted into the Earth. This is to prevent the body from always vibrating on a higher vibration than it's normally supposed to.

Guided Meditation: A meditation, usually led by another party, that assists you with reaching a meditative state.

Higher-Self: The part of us that exists in the etheric, and that feeds information and experiences to the soul. The higher-self is connected to both the physical body and the universe, via the soul.

Higher Side: The space in between Earth (lower vibration) and the Other Side. This can be called many different names, but this is where our higher-selves roam free. When we raise our vibrations, such as in meditation, we raise them to this astral plane.

House 1: The House of Self. This house represents the self and personality in the astrological chart. Its zodiac sign is Aries, and its natural planetary ruler is Mars.

House 10: The House of Status. This house represents reputation and career in the astrological chart. Its zodiac sign is Capricorn, and its natural planetary ruler is Saturn.

House 11: The House of Community. This house represents ambitions, aspirations, friendships, and associations in the astrological chart. Its zodiac sign is Aquarius, and its natural planetary ruler is Uranus.

House 12: The House of the Subconscious. In the astrological chart, this house represents the hidden self, the unknown, the unconscious. Its zodiac sign is Pisces, and its natural planetary ruler is Neptune.

House 2: The House of Money/Possessions. This house represents self-worth, possessions, and money matters in the astrological chart. Its zodiac sign is Taurus, and its natural planetary ruler is Venus.

House 3: The House of Communication. In the astrological chart, this house represents communication. Its zodiac sign is Gemini, and its natural planetary ruler is Mercury.

House 4: The House of Home. In the astrological chart, this house signifies home, family, and roots. Its zodiac sign is Cancer, and its natural planetary ruler is the moon.

House 5: The House of Enjoyment. This house signifies pleasure, romance, and creativity in the astrological chart. Its zodiac sign is Leo, and its natural planetary ruler is the Sun.

House 6: The House of Tasks. This house represents work, service, quality, and health in the astrological chart. Its zodiac sign is Virgo, and its natural planetary ruler is Mercury.

House 7: The House of Marriage. This house represents one-on-one relationships in the astrological chart. Its zodiac sign is Libra, and its natural planetary ruler is Venus.

House 8: The House of Transformation and Healing. In the astrological chart, this house signifies transformation and healing. Its zodiac sign is Scorpio, and its natural planetary ruler is Pluto.

House 9: The House of Ideas. This house signifies spirituality, philosophy, dreams, and visions in the astrological chart.

Its zodiac sign is Sagittarius, and its natural planetary ruler is Jupiter.

Hypnosis: A technique for putting one into a more open and suggestible state of concentration where the subject is more open to receiving messages and life-changing information.

Imum Coeli: Also called IC (lower heavens) and Nadir, is one of four important angles in the birth chart. It signifies our roots. It also symbolizes foundations, the beginnings in life, inherited experiences, security, and home and family life. It is the opposite of the Midheaven or MC.

Incarnate: This is when a soul has chosen to be born into a life, usually on Earth, but can also include other planets and galaxies, as well as different places and times.

Infinity Number: Numerological twin flame number that symbolizes divinity and eternity. This is the number eight. When turned on its side, it is the infinity symbol with power energy.

Journeying: A form of meditation where the vibration is raised with a specific purpose and intention.

Jupiter: This planet represents expansion and good fortune in the astrological chart.

Left Brain: The side of the brain that is more methodical and analytical.

Leo: Sign of generosity, impulsiveness, magnetism, and forcefulness.

Libra: Sign of intuition, perceptiveness, impartiality, and harmony.

Life Path Number: In numerology, this number is calculated by adding up the numbers of your birthdate until you reach a single digit. Its meaning goes beyond indicating personality, it also reveals who you are as a person, the things that matter most to you and often what challenges you will face.

Mars: The planet that represents desire in the astrological chart.

Master Builder Number: Numerological twin flame number that indicates a building up of lessons for soul progression. This is the number twenty-two. This is double the Master Twin Flame Number.

Master Teacher Number: Numerological twin flame number that indicates the teaching aspect of the twin flame relationship. This is the number thirty-three. Both twins learn and teach what they have learned on their path of soul progression.

Master Twin Flame Number: Numerological twin flame number that is associated with the ideal of twins. This is the number eleven. Not only does one plus one equal two, but each digit represents a Pillar of Twin Flames. These pillars are like bookends, and their energy stems from the Fibonacci sequence.

Masters: These are a type of spirit guide with a higher understanding and a limitless capacity for teaching, understanding, thought, compassion, and assistance. Jesus is often considered to be a master.

Meditation: This is when the physical body is purposely raising from the natural vibration to a higher vibration.

Meditative State: The state in which the etheric body is in a higher vibration than its natural one.

Medium: A person who can communicate with souls who have transitioned from life on Earth.

Mercury: The planet that represents communication style in the astrological chart.

Metaphysics: The study of the nature of human experiences that are intangible, nonphysical, or spiritual. These experiences cannot be detected or measured by our natural physical senses, research, or technology.

Midheaven: Also called the Medium Coeli (upper heavens) or MC, is one of four important angles in the birth chart. It indicates career, status, life goals, aspirations, and reputation. It is the opposite of the IC, or Imum Coeli.

Moon: Represents the emotions and emotional body, also symbolizes women in general.

Mutable: Quality that is versatile as part of the synastry of the astrological chart.

Neptune: In the astrological chart, this planet represents spirituality and psychic ability.

Numerology: The study of numbers to determine their influence on one's life, health, and liveliness.

Numerology Chart: In numerology, a chart that contains all the numeric definitions that describe an influence on one's life.

Oneness Number: Numerological twin flame number that indicates both energetic and soul oneness between the twins. This is the number one.

Opposition: In astrology, this means two celestial bodies oppose one another.

Other Side: Also called, "Summerland," "heaven," and "home," among other names, this is the destination of the soul when it exits its current incarnate lifetime, and where discarnate souls choose to remain.

Past Life Regression: Using hypnosis or guided meditation, this methodology helps to retrieve soul memories of lives previously lived or experienced. This information usually comes from either the soul itself or the Akashic Records.

Past Lives: Existences through with the soul incarnates into physical form to learn lessons.

Pisces: Sign of sensitivity, mysticism, loyalty, gentility, and shyness.

Pluto: This planet represents transformation, renewal, and elimination in the astrological chart.

Polarity: In astrology, this describes the relationship between two opposite signs of the zodiac.

Quintile: In astrology, this promotes creativity.

Race: This refers to a person's genetics and physicality, such as skin color, eye color or bone structure.

Raised Vibration: A higher vibration than the natural one that the body maintains. This is attained by purposely raising the vibration or working in the higher vibrational realms, such as the Higher Side or the Other Side.

Record: Your individual soul's energy that exists within the Akashic Records.

Reincarnation: The concept that the eternal soul will return to physical form repeatedly to learn lessons found within its soul blueprint.

Right Brain: The side of the brain that is more artistic, intuitive, emotional, and free-spirited.

Runner: The twin who cannot handle the intensity of any or all parts of the twin flame relationship. This role can change between the twins at any given time.

Sagittarius: Sign of directness, outspokenness, honesty and truth-seeking.

Saturn: In the astrological chart, this planet represents ambition, caution, organization and facing your fears.

Scorpio: Sign of intensity, loyalty, emotional awareness, and a natural capacity for romantic relations.

Semi Square: In astrology, this indicates a mildly irritating relationship.

Semisextile: In astrology, this indicates a mildly supportive relationship.

Separating Aspect: In the astrological chart, this represents the orb of the aspect between two planets as it increases over time.

Sesquiquadrate: In astrology, this indicates success.

Sextile: In astrology, this signifies support.

Soul: The infinite, boundless, divine entity created by God.

Soul Blueprint: The design created by the soul through which we plan which lessons to learn and all the ways this learning is accomplished. It contains the life plan for your existence.

Soul Evolution: To educate the soul through experience and learning to evolve to the higher levels of consciousness.

Souliverse: The universe of like souls that surround you.

Soul mate: A like soul whose purpose is to help you progress with soul evolution and allow you to assist them with their soul evolution.

Spirit: A discarnate soul who has transitioned from a life, usually on Earth, and exists on the Other Side.

Spiritual DNA: The divine energy and material makeup that is the core of the creation of the soul.

Square: In astrology, this creates friction.

Sun: Represents the essential self. Also symbolizes men in general.

Synastry: The comparison of two birth charts to determine compatibility. This comparison generally looks at the position of planets and houses in the astrological chart. It can also include various polarities, qualities and elements that can help further define the twin flame relationship.

Taurus: Sign of building, determination, and willpower.

Teachers: Guides whose main purpose or method of assisting is to teach us lessons.

Telepathy: The act of communication between minds using only thoughts not words.

Trine: In astrology, this means bringing opportunities and assisting.

Twin Flame Astrology: The study of the astrological birth charts, their similarities, their differences, and their synastry as one way to prove the twin flame relationship.

Twin Flame Cord: The cord that contains the spiritual DNA that created the souls and divinely connects the twin flames.

Twin Flame Life Path Number: In numerology, this number is calculated by adding up the individual life path numbers of each twin down to a single digit. This number indicates the overall goal for the twins in this lifetime.

Twin Flame Numerology: The study of numbers to determine compatibility and as one way to prove the twin flame relationship.

Twin Flame Polarity: Indicates the balance between the divine feminine (yin) and the divine masculine (yang) in the twin flame relationship.

Twin Flame Stages: Stages of growth, release, learning, and coming together of both twins in the relationship. These stages are designed to bring the twins both closer together and further on their path to soul evolution.

Twin Flames: The other half of your divine soul that shares the same spiritual DNA and soul blueprint with you.

Universal Number: Numerological twin flame number that symbolizes connection to the universe. This is the number seven.

Uranus: This planet signifies originality, independence, and inventiveness in the astrological chart.

Veil: Energetic and etheric curtain that separates the sentient (Earth) plane from the etheric plane, or the Other Side.

Venus: The planet that represents love in the astrological chart.

Vibration: The frequency at which your body naturally moves.

Virgo: Sign of practicality, dependability, and perfectionism.

Water: The element that represents sensitivity, imagination, and emotions.

Yang: Negative polarity in the synastry of the astrological chart. Also called the divine masculine polarity.

Yin: Positive polarity in the synastry of the astrological chart. Also called the divine feminine polarity.

Bibliography

Columbia University Irving Medical Center, The Pancreas Center. "The Pancreas and Its Functions." Accessed July 1, 2021. https://columbiasurgery.org/pancreas /pancreas-and-its-functions.

Dvorsky, George. "Fifteen Uncanny Examples of the Golden Ratio in Nature." Gizmodo. Last updated February 20, 2013. https://io9.gizmodo.com/15-uncanny-examples-of -the-golden-ratio-in-nature-5985588.

Eldridge, Lynne. "An Overview of the Thymus Gland." Very-Well Health. Last updated June 24, 2020. https://www .verywellhealth.com/thymus-gland-overview-4582270.

Encyclopedia Britannica. "Pythagoreanism." Accessed February 2018. https://www.britannica.com/topic/number -symbolism/Pythagoreanism.

Ermith, Jen. "The Records of Many Names." Last updated July 13, 2011. https://akashictransformations.com/the -records-of-many-names/.

Ghose, Tia. "What is the Fibonacci Sequence?" LiveScience. Last updated October 24, 2018. https://www.livescience .com/37470-fibonacci-sequence.html.

Johns Hopkins Medicine. "Adrenal Glands." Accessed July 1, 2021. https://www.hopkinsmedicine.org/health /conditions-and-diseases/adrenal-glands.

Kotsos, Tania. "What Is the Law of Attraction and How Does It Work?" Accessed July 1, 2021. https://www.mind-your-reality.com/law_of _attraction.html.

Merriam-Webster. "Astrology." Accessed July 1, 2021. https://www.merriam- webster.com/dictionary/astrology.

Society for Endocrinology, The. "Where Is My Pituitary Gland?" Accessed February 2018. https://www .yourhormones.info/glands/pituitary-gland/.

Web MD. "Hypothyroidism." Last updated August 26, 2020. https://www.webmd.com/women/hypothyroidism -underactive-thyroid-symptoms-causes-treatments#1.

Wilson, Colin. *The Occult: A History*. New York: Random House, 1971.

You and Your Hormones. "Pituitary Gland." Accessed February 2018. https://www.yourhormones.info/glands /pituitary-gland/.

To Write to the Author

If you wish to contact the author or would like more information about this book, please write to the author in care of Llewellyn Worldwide Ltd., and we will forward your request. Both the author and publisher appreciate hearing from you and learning of your enjoyment of this book and how it has helped you. Llewellyn Worldwide Ltd. cannot guarantee that every letter written to the author can be answered, but all will be forwarded. Please write to:

Leslie Sampson
℅ Llewellyn Worldwide
2143 Wooddale Drive
Woodbury, MN 55125-2989

Please enclose a self-addressed stamped envelope for reply,
or $1.00 to cover costs. If outside the U.S.A., enclose
an international postal reply coupon.

Many of Llewellyn's authors have websites with additional information and resources. For more information, please visit our website at http://www.llewellyn.com.